From Illusion
to
Enlightenment

From Illusion
to
Enlightenment

MICHAEL J. ROADS

SIX DEGREES PUBLISHING GROUP

PORTLAND • OREGON • USA

FROM ILLUSION TO ENLIGHTENMENT

FIRST SIX DEGREES PUBLISHING GROUP SOFTCOVER EDITION
February 2017

ISBN: 978-1-942497-24-0
EBook ISBN: 978-1-942497-25-7

LCCN: 2017932264

Six Degrees Publishing Group
5331 S. W. Macadam Avenue, Suite 258
Portland, OR 97239

Content includes selected poems from *The Prophet* by Kahlil Gibran, original copyright 1923, 1951.

Published in the USA

1 3 7 9 10 8 6 4 2

Dedication & Tribute

THIS BOOK IS A TRIBUTE TO KAHLIL GIBRAN as a mark of my respect
and admiration for him. Born on the 6th January, 1883, in Lebanon, he
died in New York City on the 10th of April, 1931, just a few years before I
was born. His body was buried in his beloved Lebanon.

During the years of my search for spiritual enlightenment, none of
the many books that I read gave me more inspiration than his great work,
The Prophet. He nurtured my growing bud of tomorrow. His style of
writing, his flair with words and the beauty and truth of his words have
stayed with me ever since I first read him . . . over forty years ago. I have
reread *The Prophet* so many times that the flow of his prose continues to
haunt me in the way that the warm summer breeze haunts my garden.

As though his writing was not enough, I still own and occasionally listen
to a CD of the late, great Irish actor Richard Harris as, with the assistance
of a choir, his evocative voice, with its wonderful lilting brogue, sings and
chants a musical rendition of *The Prophet*.

Please be assured that in no way am I attempting to copy or imitate his style of writing. I could not, even if I wanted to! He is inimitable. This book is my tribute to his poetic genius with words . . . to his impeccable shadows of wordless wisdom. I am almost lost in admiration for his profound and innate ability to inspire and impart Truth within me by plucking the strings of my heart, thus enabling me to connect with my own deep-soul wisdom at the level of Oneness.

Written on Gibran's grave are the words: "I am alive like you, and I am standing beside you. Close your eyes and look around you, and you will see me in front of you."

While Kahlil Gibran has undoubtedly moved on with his life, and could not be found at his graveside, he is saying that we should not look into death for those who have passed on, but that we should look for them within life. All is possible within the framework of a spiritually opened heart and mind.

CONTENTS

CONTENTS

Appreciation & Thanks

I ALWAYS ENJOY WRITING OF MY APPRECIATION and gratitude to those people who pave my books with the golden touch of their talents.

At the top of the list is my beloved wife, Carolyn. She is my number one critic and, happily, my number one fan. She is the first reader of my books, so she is the first to encounter my errors with words, or my in-articulation. I often feel a degree of pride in my ability to create a rather poetic sentence, or a super articulate paragraph in describing a difficult subject. So I am very humbled when she points out a few word changes that seriously improve the whole structure of what I was attempting to write. And she does this constantly in that first reading of my new manuscripts. So thank you, my darling, for this and the thousands of other daily reasons that I *Love* having you in my life.

My sincere thanks also go to Brian and Theresa Longhurst for their very valued ability to edit my use of the English language. Brian suggests removal and replacement of some of my words in the manner of a master chess player moving and removing the pieces on a chess board. And Theresa, the master of contextual grammar and punctuation, puts in – or takes out – the colons, semicolons, apostrophes, commas, spacings, periods, and more, where they correctly should be, or shouldn't be, as the case may be.

My deep and sincere thanks also go the delightful, helpful, thoughtful, insightful, kind and courteous Denise, of Six Degrees Publishing. As my publisher and final editor, it also helps immensely that she enjoys my writings!

Also to my daughter, Tracey, thank you for being so patient with me all the many times I call up the stairs from my study . . . "Tracey, help. I've got a computer problem!" She willingly and unfailingly sorts out the problem.

To the ever-increasing numbers of you intelligent and inner-growing people who read my books, thank you. You are my reason for writing. May you thrive and prosper and keep on buying and reading my books!

To all the people who have been both true friends and important catalysts in my life, a multitude of thanks in a multitude of languages to a multitude of people throughout the first half of this, my ongoing life!

And last but never least, to Pan and all the many metaphysical Beings who smile on me so very patiently . . . my endless, undying gratitude.

Introduction

MANY OF MY BOOKS are about my metaphysical journeying. This book is a departure from that theme. It is a book about enlightenment, about an enlightened way of living, although it is extremely difficult to describe this elusive state of consciousness. As soon as I say what it is . . . it is not that! It is a bit like attempting to pin a shadow to sunlight. We know what sunlight is and we know what shadows are, but it is not so easy to grasp that it is the shadows that allow us to know sunlight and sunlight that ultimately defines the shadows. They appear separate, but they are one. Paradoxically, while light does not have the physical properties to cast a shadow, it is light that creates shadows. I have observed that metaphysically light actually does cast a shadow: the more intense the light, the deeper the metaphysical shadow.

I am a spiritually enlightened man. I do not think that I am spiritually enlightened, I *know* it. This book is a result of the regular question; "Do you have a book that is about your teachings?" Actually, no, I did not! It was not something that I wanted to do . . . mainly because of misleading words.

For example, we have a very common term 'awake'. A lot of people who claim to be awakened are still firmly embedded in the illusion. I can only assume this term 'awake' is somehow a replacement or addition to the term 'aware'. Being aware of their spirituality, aware that the way life is normally perceived and experienced is all illusion. While this 'awake' perception of life has many virtues, it is a long way from being spiritually enlightened . . . if anything at all is a long way from it . . . which it is not!

You see what I mean? As soon as I write about what spiritual enlightenment is, or is not, I get caught in the cobweb of words. Words and language were created for a world of separation, for the illusion, rather than a holistic world reality of connectedness. Despite this, I can clearly state that spiritual enlightenment has nothing whatsoever to do with personality. And if you are attached to any belief at all, you are unenlightened. If you argue for your truth, or have a need to prove your words to others, you are still playing games in the deep shadows of illusion.

Although in our linear time you can fix a date for when you became enlightened, it perpetrates an illusion. Enlightenment is not held in linear time, it resides in the eternal moment. Enlightenment is never in your past, it is in your *now*. Like the eternal flower symbolised by the lotus, enlightenment continues to unfold and express in the moment, for it is not a static state. The person who wrote, 'Before I was enlightened I chopped wood and carried water, and after I was enlightened I chopped wood and carried water,' was attempting to convey the impression that nothing changes . . . yet it does . . . and it does not!

I think a more enlightening way to say it would be, 'Before I was enlightened I chopped wood and carried water. (Actually, I did!) After I was enlightened I chopped wood and carried water . . . effortlessly!' (And so it was.) To me, this conveys that while nothing changes, everything changes.

Having written many books about my metaphysical journeys, I would like to clarify that metaphysical journeying does not require a person to be enlightened. Equally, metaphysical journeying is not actually a path to spiritual enlightenment, nor was it my path to my enlightenment. However, for me, metaphysical journeying was, and is, almost as natural as is physical journeying. My metaphysical journeys preceding my enlightenment were nothing like my current metaphysical journeys as an enlightened man.

My early journeys so often led me into emotional pain and many painful confrontations with my own inadequacies. The metaphysical journeys that I write about nowadays and are published in some of my books are hugely life enriching. However, having said this, I need to add that my early journeys were integral to my own spiritual enlightenment for they expressed the essential me. Simply put, as a mystic, this was me on my path.

Of course, as soon as I say 'path' I am again straying from Truth with words created in illusion, for there is no path and the no-path is going nowhere. On the other hand we are no-self on the no-path going nowhere, so we might as well create a few fun illusions along the way. Okay, I joke!

In the pages of this book I am taking a look at many of the issues that people encounter in everyday life. I share a more enlightened way of viewing them, and offer my suggestions on how to easily jump over these hurdles, for they are obstacles that bring many people to needless pain and trauma.

As always in my books, I place a capital letter in front of each word I wish to *powerfully* emphasise. Obviously there is a huge difference between transformational Change and a change of clothes! Or the Truth of Life and a truth that is personal. Or 'I Love my wife' and 'I love my car!'

And so it goes. As a right-brain dominant character, I like a story, so all the Truths and insights that lead toward spiritual enlightenment are embedded in a very simple storyline. And who knows, maybe we will all grow in the process of writing and reading? We will become One in timelessness, for just as the reader connects with the writer, so the writer connects with the reader . . . thus may we all connect with eternal Truth.

Michael J. Roads
Queensland, Oz.

...ONE...

The Art of Listening

You cannot think your way into the moment. You can only think your way out of it. To listen, you have to be consciously established in the moment.
—Michael J. Roads

THE SUN IS A WASH of pale, early morning colour as I walk slowly through a section of my garden. I sigh. Today could prove to be a rather taxing day. I am expecting a few visitors who wish to talk with me about the meaning of life. Life! I can remember when my life was my own, but something sneaky came in with enlightenment, something that seems to think that I am no longer the personal property of me, something that seems to think that I have become public property . . . or at least, the public that is interested in such things that I teach. I have been assured that these are rather important people – whatever that means – so while my refusal would be rather churlish, at least I was able to choose the place where we will meet . . . my home and garden. I am known to relish my precious home time.

1

My wife, Carolyn, and I are busy people, travelling to many countries each year, so for me to agree to this meeting is rather unusual. I have a very sympathetic organising team, who consider me to be a rather busy man. According to the time I/we put into travelling and presenting my 5-Day Intensives around the world, and also writing books when at home, with the occasional webinars thrown in, I guess I am. Nevertheless, busy is a state of consciousness, and I do not have that fluster of busyness within me. So while I am constantly occupied with busy, inside I am really very relaxed. Despite this, I am hoping they will not be superficial people, full of self-importance, because if they are this will probably end rather quickly. I have been assured that they are not, so I choose to trust this assurance.

A wistful smile tugs at my lips as I consider the irony of my life. I am a fairly private man who has somehow become fairly public. Oh, I have no one to blame, only myself, and I know that I am blameless. Life has its way! I am a man who teaches the wisdom of Love without conditions, so I choose to unconditionally accept how the day will unfold. Meanwhile I have a little time before they arrive.

Standing close to our waterlily pond, I watch the large red dragonflies as they skim the water's surface before settling on a flower. Skimming the surface, I muse. This is how so many people live their lives . . . just skimming the surface. It works for dragonflies, but not for humans. We need to plumb the depths. And this is my passion, my speciality. I love exploring the deeper Mystery of life, not so much to understand it, but to *experience* it. In my metaphysical body I explore the multiverse. I have become a conscious metaphysical traveller. I use the term *conscious* simply because everyone travels in their astral body at night while sleeping, albeit comparatively few do so while conscious and aware of the process.

Even so, my metaphysical travelling is rather different. I am awake in my physical body, not sleeping. I have learned that I can vacate my physical body with as much ease as physically vacating a car. I smile . . . easier, in fact, than from some of these new, low, modern, city cars. Metaphysically leaving your body entails a deep level of conscious inner relaxation. Many people consider that they *are* their body, but this is an error. We are not our physical bodies; we are not even truly physical, we are pure metaphysical Beings. I consider that, metaphysically, the average person – if they exist! –

is about three times larger than their physical body. If a person is highly spiritually developed, the metaphysical body can be as much as ten times larger than their physical body.

I was taught at school that the body contains consciousness, and to a degree, this is true, but it is not the whole truth. It would be more accurate to say that the metaphysical body envelops, contains, and fills the whole physical body with its metaphysical substance. In other words, we are not in-body people as nearly everyone seems to believe; we are out-of-body Beings having an in-body experience that we call life.

So what is life? The fleeting experience that most people have of life is just a mere glimpse of something far, far greater. We are fully equipped to have a far greater experience than most people currently enjoy, but life is in the moment . . . and people are seldom in this exclusive zone of pure, conscious creation.

I glance at my wristwatch . . . hmm, ten minutes to eight, almost time for my visitors. I walk to the house, up the outside steps and onto our verandah. Once again, I smile in pleasure. I long ago converted our once-upon-a-time swimming pool into a fish pond, and I watch as a startled water dragon plonks into the water. He must be a stranger; ours are rather tame. A visiting male perhaps, eying up our resident females. This living pond with its goldfish, red swords and other fish, gives us so much more pleasure than an occasional swim in a sterile swimming pool. We also breed the Great Eastern Water Dragons to release around the various ponds; pure reptilian cuteness . . . especially the babies!

"Your visitors phoned ahead to say that they will be here in a few minutes," my lovely wife Carolyn tells me as I enter the house. "If you like I'll fill the hot water jug ready for when they arrive?"

I nod. "Yes please. Tea or coffee seems to be the traditional way of greeting people, so why not. It's a good ice breaker."

"And Michael . . . be nice," she tells me.

I chuckle. "It's okay, I'm resigned to my fate."

Carolyn is very aware that we both enjoy our private time at home when we are not travelling the world, but she felt that this session with these people was important. I trust her judgement, so I accepted it. The "be nice" remark was a warning to behave, as I have been known to come on just a wee bit strong when I feel the occasion demands it. I have never been impressed by people who request a visit, claiming that they want to listen to what I have to say about life, and then talk non-stop about themselves for the entire allotted time. But as I implied, it happens but rarely.

The bell at our front door rings vigorously, and I smile. I like people who are not afraid to announce their arrival. It goes with strong self-esteem. Some tap the door so gently with their knuckles, or ding the bell softly once. To me, this immediately suggests shyness and timidity, along with poor self-worth. But, as Carolyn has often said, maybe it simply means that they are polite!

Carolyn opens the door and ushers in five people, three men and two women. I approach them, noting the keen enthusiasm on their faces as they greet me.

"Hi, I'm Todd. I'm a psychologist . . . !" he begins before I cut him off.

"Please, just your names will do me. I really do not want to know what you do for a living."

As a result I shake hands with first Todd, a short, open-faced man with a built-in smile, fair hair, blue eyes, and a strong build, and probably in his early forties. Anita comes next, a slim, brunette with a happy expression, and an easy engaging manner. She is in her early twenties. Marsha, thirty-something, is of a more solid build, very dark hair, and is more serious as she shakes hands. Bill is very tall, very lean as he looms over me. A serious expression on his face and with piercing blue eyes. He is a similar age to Peter, the third man, who would be in his late forties. Peter is also tall, with a strong body and a stubborn set to his jaw. He is also darker in complexion, and with an edge of uncertainty about him.

Todd and Bill shake my hand as though they are delighted to meet me; Peter's handshake holds a lot of hesitancy. Not so with the ladies, strong handshakes and big smiles. All in all they have created a good impression. Energetically, I can see this should go well. The potential is strong.

As soon as Carolyn has introduced herself, and while the people are relaxing in her loving energy, I go to switch the kettle on. We both know that people relax better with Carolyn than with me. It's an energy thing. My energy is strong, apparently; initially too strong for some people. They need time to get used to it. Carolyn, on the other hand, is so kind and loving and disarming and welcoming she could relax a mad bull. So she gets them into chairs while I call out for tea or coffee orders from the kitchen.

When everyone is comfortably seated with their drinks in hand, I give them all my most affable smile. "So what exactly is the reason for this visit? As I understand it, you want to ask me about the difference between an enlightened way of life compared with the normal everyday approach to life. Is this the gist of it? Maybe you can explain a bit more."

Todd, the first to speak and clearly unintimidated by me – I like that – gives an explanation. "Without sharing our occupational qualifications, let me just say that we are all part of a larger network that enables us to assist and motivate a great many people whose lives are a serious struggle. We give them all the usual everyday assistance, and this helps, but studying other people's problems has shown us that we have the same problems that they do, although thankfully, to a lesser degree. So a few of us discussed this and decided that we wanted to talk with a person who has an inside track on life. Someone who has the wisdom and vision . . . and, er, deeper experience of life that we clearly lack."

Anita comes in strongly. "We want to get an enlightened insight into life. Into what life is, what it means, and most of all, how to live it. To this end we have made a list of topics that we would like you to talk about. And to be fully honest, we were rather excited when you agreed to do this with us. So thank you very much. And I apologise that the list kept growing longer and longer every time we looked at it and added some more!"

I chuckled. "In that case, it's just as well we did not delay this for another week. It would have become an endless list."

"Oh . . . and do you mind if I record it?" Marsha asks.

"It's probably just as well that you do," I said. "But please remember that what I speak about and say is not necessarily what you will hear."

Marsha looks as bewildered as the others. "Er . . . I don't understand. What do you mean?" she asks.

I smile. "Okay, here we go, the first session is about to begin."

"But, er, we have not suggested a subject yet," Peter says, looking rather exasperated.

"No . . . you haven't, but first of all you need to know exactly what I mean when I ask you to *listen*. I expect you to listen to what I am saying, not rely on the recorder for my words. When I am speaking to you – like now – I am speaking in the moment. If you are listening to me, you are not thinking – and without a doubt, you *are* thinking! People think as they listen, but when they do this they are not truly listening, they are hearing. Today, most people don't know the difference between hearing and listening. Let me put it this way; you can think your way out of the moment, but you cannot think your way into it. When I speak, I speak only in the moment. This means that if you are listening to me, you are inner-silent. In this way, we connect. However, if you are thinking while I am speaking, we do not connect, so you will forget most of what you heard while not listening." I smile at them. "This however, is considered normal. Beware of normality!"

"But... surely if I hear your words I will remember them," Todd protests. "This is part of my training."

"Oh sure. You might well remember a small conversation, but during one of my Intensives I talk in one and a half hour sessions pretty much all day for five days. Many participants by the end of the first day are exhausted, simply because they have no idea how to relax and listen. They don't teach this in schools, so kids grow up establishing a false relationship with knowledge and information. Even adults do not seem to realise that information is just exactly what the word implies: in-formation, unformed, unrealised, not yet actualised. And all for the sake of something as simple as listening."

Peter nods sagely. "Okay, I confess that I am thinking almost all the time. But, how do I stop this? How do I get away from my thoughts to listen?"

I give him a big smile. "Now that, my friend, is an intelligent question. First you need to accept that most people have non-stop, queued-up thoughts. They run at about two to three hundred words a minute, even faster for a busy mind, which all add up to around sixty thousand thoughts a day of pure unadulterated nonsense. Animals don't do this!

"Even worse, the thoughts that people think today have almost the same content of anxiety, worries and fears in them that they had a thousand lifetimes ago. Sure, the language changes, but not the basic human content. The reasons for the anxiety and fears change, but it is still the same old anxiety and fears of survival that fill most people's everyday thoughts."

Marsha looks thoughtful. "So how does listening change this?"

"Listen, Marsha, listen. Listening connects you with the eternal moment. In *the moment* is unconditional Love. In the moment is conscious intelligence. In the moment is freedom. In the moment is peace. In the moment is trust. All these are in the moment . . . *and they never leave it.* People are never in the moment, or at least so seldom that it is a rare event. Can you imagine a humanity that is consciously connected in the moment? Seriously, can you?"

Marsha shakes her head. "Not consciously connected, no, I can't. It would be . . . incredible, momentous."

"You're right. It would be momentous indeed."

"When you speak like this, of something that none of us has ever even considered, it . . . well it makes the topics of our questions seem rather trite," Bill says, in a subdued voice.

He seems to be the quiet one, the thoughtful one, maybe the deeper one. I can hope!

"Don't let it concern you. Let's be fair and considerate here. This body is eighty years of age. I became spiritually enlightened when this body was forty-nine and three months, so I have been around and growing in consciousness for quite a while. And, quite honestly, I plan to be around for a long time yet. I consider that this body is just a few years over middle age. Age to me equates with wisdom, not infirmity. So please, don't be shy of your subject matter. I will not be judging it. It is possible that you may go into overwhelm at how much you don't know, but that is good. It's humbling, and we all need regular doses of being humbled. I get deeply humbled travelling the world when I realise just how many people truly Love the person I am . . . warts and all."

By now the five people are relaxing and smiling. The edges of anxiety are fading away, and they probably realise that my reputation is fiercer than the reality. As Carolyn often says, 'He's just a big pussy cat.' Purr, purr!

I continue. "All of Nature listens. Every hunting animal, every hunted animal, they listen . . . they are in the moment. No animal can think its way out of the moment, the place of life, of energy, of power, of its greatest potential. We are the same. Everything that we spiritually aspire to is with us in the moment. By listening we connect."

"How did you know to even begin to listen, because it's not common knowledge?" Bill says.

"I had read in books the possibility of listening to Nature. Years ago I wanted to listen to the wisdom of a certain river, so I knew that I had to learn to listen. Every day, for a few minutes or a few hours, I sat by the river doing my best to listen to the silence of the river. Months and years passed, and all I heard was the mocking echo of my own thoughts. I heard the passing traffic not far away, tractors in nearby paddocks, people shouting, calling to each other, birds' calls . . . everything except the river. One year, two years, three years, and I refused to give up. That was not an option. During the fourth year I had fleeting touches of connection, but late in the fifth year it all unfolded. The river communicated with me within the silence, becoming my teacher. Over the next few years it taught me so much."

"Wow! Like what?" Anita asks. "Whatever could a river teach a man?"

I laugh. "If you get me going on this we might not get through your long list," I reply.

Sharing a quick glance, they all decide that this is more important. "Please, let's follow this lead and see where it takes us," Anita asks.

. . . TWO . . .

Newness and Sameness

Do not try to put my words together in a way that make sense for you. That is a process of reducing newness to sameness, and this is what most people do. It does not work. People live lives of endless sameness, and to feel safe, anything that is new and does not fit the sameness box has to be understood. But this understanding all takes place in the sameness box, so newness is now no longer new, it has been reshaped to fit the sameness box.

—Michael J. Roads

"Okay, just as you wish. I'll keep it brief. One day when I was listening to the river communicating, it asked me if I saw the river as *new* in every moment. That really floored me, because I saw the river as the *same* river every day. If I was to throw a piece of wood in the water, and follow it as it flowed with the river, then that would be the same section of river that I would be following. But I was sitting on some rocks, and as the river flowed past me it was the epitome of newness in every moment, yet it looked exactly the same to me. Right there and then, I knew that I had to learn to see the newness of the river. But I wasn't sure how to do it.

9

"Of course, despite having asked me, it gave me no clue! I decided that the best approach was to see my late wife and my kids as new in every moment." I smile whimsically. "Much easier said than done. For month after month I did my best to see the newness in them, and for month after month they seemed to be aggravatingly the same as always. I was getting nowhere fast. This went on for almost a year, when one morning just as I first woke up, I had a surge of insight. I suddenly *knew* that only the *newness in me* could see the newness in my wife and kids. I had been looking from the sameness in me, seeing only the sameness in them."

"I'm amazed that you discover such things," Anita says.

"Anyway, I began then to search for the newness in me, and I have to say that this took me about another year. Eventually, I found it. Once I discovered the newness in me, the newness in my wife and kids was so obvious. It was there every day, literally every moment. Life changed. Of course, this all began with the river, so I went back to the river and saw, felt, and experienced its newness in every moment. At this stage the river began to flow through me, rather than just follow the river bed."

"How is that possible?" Anita burst out.

"Well . . . to be accurate, the physical river continued to follow the normal course of the river, but the *energy* of the river, the metaphysical river simply flowed through the energy-field I am. It felt natural, to tell the truth."

"Oh my God, what people say about you is true. I thought it would have to be all exaggerations," Anita said in a daze. "We were told that once you began talking a whole new world would be presented to us, that nothing is the way it seems."

I chuckle. "In all truth, nothing *is* as it seems. Life is so much more simple than the intellect can grasp, and a zillion times greater than small thinking can conceive. But, we spend a lot of time being educated in how to think small and compartmentalised. Oh, many people do manage some very lofty thoughts, but mostly even those thoughts are confined to the illusion. Most people think their lives into complex situations, assuming that life is complicated. Nothing could be further from the Truth. Life is vast, but within that immensity there runs a connecting thread of simplicity. Never think that simple is stupid, because life clearly demonstrates that simple is powerful. All the great Truths are simple and powerful. However . . . it is as it is. So now I have shared this, I insist that we come up with one of your subjects.

Anita glances around. "Well, I don't know about the rest of you, but the tidy order of our topics has been rendered obsolete for the moment. I, for one, would like you to expand on newness and, er, sameness. If that's okay with you?"

I nod. "Of course, if it meets mutual agreement."

Everyone nods obligingly.

I sigh. This is going to be a long haul. "You will realise that everything I talk about is connected with everything I talk about . . . of course! There is no subject that you can come up with that is disconnected from everything else in life. It is all One. The only disconnection that we have to contend with is the human disconnection from Truth. And that's another paradox. We are always connected with Truth, but if we are not consciously aware of our connection, it equates to being about as efficient as if we were disconnected."

"Er . . . I don't understand," Peter says, looking aggravated.

"Yep . . . and that's yet another human problem; the constant need to understand. Please, just put your need to understand on hold for a while . . . and listen. *Listen*, do you get it? Just open your hearts and listen. *Be* with it. If you are listening there are no questions. When there are no questions you are in the place where the answers are; the answers to the unthought and unasked questions. I call it the place of *inner knowing*. So . . . let's now address the issue of newness and sameness."

"I'm lost," Peter says, irritated and aggravated.

"Actually, being intellectually lost is very creative territory. Stay lost. But listen . . . *listen!* Don't try to put my words together in a way that make sense for you. That is a process of reducing newness to sameness, and this is what most people do. It does not work. People live lives of endless sameness, and to feel safe, anything that is new and does not fit the sameness box has to be understood. But this understanding all takes place in the sameness box, so newness is now no longer new, it has been reshaped to fit the sameness box.

"This is what they did to us at school. We must all learn to fit into the sameness box, often to the point where the kids wear a sameness uniform.

By the time we leave school we have lost our childhood connection with our birthright of conscious intelligence. Instead, we have been thoroughly conditioned into the subconscious intellect. Anyway, I digress, although the subconscious and sameness hold hands very tightly."

"It seems you are talking about the things that happen in our overall lives of which we have no true awareness. Is this right?" Todd asks.

I nod. "That sums it up nicely. We have two distinctly different states of consciousness in us, both of which are running all the time. We have a true reality of the consciousness of the moment, and simultaneously we have the illusion of how we think life is. The former escapes our conscious awareness, the latter is considered normality. In this way we each create our own personal world reality. All the collective personal world realities within a nation are held within an overall consensual reality of that nation, all fitting nicely together in a way that the people of this nation agree that this is how it is. Finally all the personal and national reality illusions are contained within a global consensual human reality. All of which define and detail the illusions in which most people live. By common agreement, the many illusionary realities are all based in sameness, while the few people who are enlightened, or of a higher consciousness, experience the newness of the moment. And both of these ways of living, my friends, are very, very different."

"So an example of a common reality could be that the past is fixed and finished and cannot be changed, while the future has not yet happened," Todd suggested. "I'm pretty sure we would all agree to that."

I smile at him. "Yes, I'm sure you would, but you would be in error. In a greater reality all time occupies the same moment, meaning that the past and future are taking place simultaneously in the moment, and thus the past can be changed as easily as the future. I do this with people during our five-day Intensives. Anything in the past that is unresolved is unresolved in this moment, and in this moment it can be changed and resolved. Simple, huh!"

"You see." Anita squeaks excitedly, "he's doing it again. Just as we sort out up from down, he shows us that they are both unreal. God, this is so challenging."

"Actually, my version of life is extremely simple, while your version does not make sense. I am known as a spiritual teacher. After many years of resisting this label, I now capitulate; I'm a spiritual teacher. But I still do not see it this way. To me, there are two ways of living life; one way works, the other way does not. The real puzzle is why about ninety-four percent of humanity live in a way that does not work, while about six percent live in a way that does. And you realise, of course, that the ninety-four percent are addicted to sameness, while the six percent live within the unfolding newness of the moment."

"So how do we live in the way of newness?" Anita asks.

"By being conscious in the moment. It is that simple," I reply.

"But I am conscious . . . what else could I be?" Anita objects.

"Be honest. In your daily life how often are you conscious of being conscious in the moment? As opposed to simply living your life immersed in thoughts and emotions. Which of these is most familiar to you?"

Anita sighs, long and deep. "When you put it like that, I'm immersed in thoughts and emotions."

"And that's okay, Anita. Many people live very rich and beneficial lives in this way; lives that contribute much to society. But unfortunately, it is a sick society simply because no matter how well we may live the illusion, it is not life supportive. Being conscious is life supportive; it is life in the moment, the place of power and Truth. It is the place of newness, of direct knowing, as opposed to merely understanding."

"Okay, er, Mr Roads, it seems we need to understand more about understanding," Todd says, with a laugh. "I think!"

"Please . . . Michael, none of this Mr Roads stuff. We are a group of friends having a chat about life."

"No, we are not. Friends, yes, I like that, but we are a group of students who have suddenly found themselves with a master. At least, that's what it feels like for me," Marsha declares.

Most heads nod, while Peter stares fixedly away from us.

And this is okay. People are more inclined to listen when they are skirting the territory of knowing that they do not know. It's a creative place. Most people are trapped in the place of thinking that they *do* know; a real quagmire. And if you attempt to rescue them they argue for staying bogged!

"We have not really finished with newness and sameness yet, but I have no doubt that they will roll around again in our continuing conversation. However, there is one observation that I would like to point out within Nature. I have a large and mostly beautiful garden . . . sometimes rendered not quite so beautiful by drought. Each year the shrubs and plants flower, and each season each flower is brand spanking new. Despite this, many gardeners see a repeat of last year's flowers. Their relationship with the flowers is based in the physical form, not in the energy of the flower. This suggests that they see through yesterday's eyes, rather than through the eyes of immediacy. All Nature sees through the eyes of immediacy, in the moment, in the place of newness. We can learn to do this, but we have to be conscious. Being conscious is the place of newness, while living our conditioned subconscious life is the place of continuing sameness. This has now become dangerous territory."

"Why is it dangerous?" Anita asks.

"Well, to put it simply, we humans have become seriously attached to more of the same. No matter how painful or uncomfortable it is, we have this mental and emotional attachment. Our dislike of change has been very well documented. We are in dangerous territory because we cannot change and remain the same. But humanity attempts to change *and* remain the same. Even in times of great adversity, when whole towns are either flooded, or destroyed by wild fires, in the aftermath, when interviewed about what they will do next, the survivors mostly say, 'I just want my old life back.' Another way of saying, I want more of the same.

"When we get habitually stuck in a way of living that repeats itself for lifetime after lifetime we cease to consciously grow. We simply move into a subconscious function mode. As unlikely as it may seem, eventually this will precipitate massive changes in Nature that will literally force us into change. We name these sorts of pressure as natural disasters, and we don't like them! Yet, the way we are now heading is toward a global disaster."

"All because we don't like change!" Peter says sceptically.

"Peter, my friend, without getting sidetracked here, you need to realise that we are a sick species. The slightest research on the Internet will reveal that every major illness is on the rise; cancer, heart attacks, strokes, diabetes, obesity, and of course, suicide, just to name a few, while there is a new case of dementia about every four to five seconds. Right now we are living on the edge of a pandemic of major, epic proportions just in mental and emotional health issues alone.

"But you did not come here to hear about this. You came to learn about the highest potential for a person, not their lowest. However, when we live in such appalling ignorance of who we are, as humanity is doing right now, trust me, we are living in *very* dangerous times."

"So who are we?" Marsha asks.

I smile. "Aha, now that's the BIG question."

...THREE...

What It Is to Be Human

So spoke the Prophet: *Fare you well, people of Orphalese.*
This day is ended. It is closing upon us even as the water-
lily upon its own tomorrow.
What was given us here we shall keep, and if it suffices not,
then again we must come together and together stretch our
hands unto the giver.
Forget not that I shall come back to you.
A little while, and my longing shall gather together dust
and foam for another body.
A little while, a moment of rest upon the wind,
and another woman shall bear me.
                                                        —Kahlil Gibran

"Who are we? What are we? We are space. Quantum physics tells us that if you were to remove the space from within every atom of our physical bodies, the whole human race could fit into an area the size of a sugar cube. They tell us that we are each more than 99.9% space. Metaphysical inquiry supports this. This includes not only humanity, but all Nature and even the planet Earth itself. All space."

"I've read about this," Todd says. "A whole lot of interesting stuff, but it doesn't make any difference regarding how we live our lives. I feel solid enough, and that is the simple fact of it. If my body gets hit, I bruise or bleed."

"Sure, but the question was, 'Who are we?' Listen to this. We are space. All space is energy, and all energy is information. Our human information is carried in our DNA. The information of every creature, everything with life, is carried in its DNA. Let's call this DNA the blueprint. So we each carry a blueprint of who we are, which is completely ignored."

"How so?" ask Marsha.

"Well, Marsha, your blueprint holds the information that you are a metaphysical Being of pure energy, ageless and tireless, as well as a physical person with a genetic code. Yet the life you live is mostly a physical one, with little to no regard for your metaphysical immortality. You also have beliefs about yourself that have no foundation in Truth. Over aeons of time, along with all humanity, we have fabricated beliefs that reduce us to mere shadows of our greater reality. Those shadows have become personalised, as in a personal reality, nationalised, as in our national realities, and finally into an overall globalised reality . . . as I mentioned earlier."

"Surely it is you who are now making something simple become very complicated and confusing," Peter accuses me.

"The only reason this appears as confusing is because you are deeply conditioned into an illusion, never having been exposed to Truth, until now. You have been blinded to Truth, unable to see it or hear it. It's rather like the Matrix movies. Life in the illusion and life outside it. You are attached to the beliefs that appear to control human life. They do not control it, they simply create uncomfortable but very familiar conditions to which you are attached and totally believe are real."

"And are you offering us a way out of the illusion?" Todd asks, quietly.

I shake my head. "To be honest, no. It takes a full five days at an Intensive for most people to let go of the illusion and begin to engage the ever-unfolding flower of Truth. This is a process, and while for some it may be slow and painful, for others it can be faster and joyous. It all depends on the depth of their emotional attachments, their openness, and where they are on their spiritual journey. To be honest, I had no intention of going this far into the depths of life. I intended it to be a session of your questions and my insights and . . . goodbye. Somewhat to my surprise, I find that you are all worth much more than that. You are people of value to other people."

Carolyn, who had been flitting around in the background, stepped in to fill the sudden silence.

"More tea, coffee, anyone?"

Most smiled and nodded, while looking rather pensive.

"Obviously we don't have five days," Marsha says. "Is there any way you could, er . . . sort of summarise all this regarding humanity?"

I smile at her. "Good thinking.

"Okay, in your full Truth you each are a magnificent, metaphysical, multidimensional, immortal Being of Love and Light. However, most people live as a mediocre, physical, three-dimensional mortal person of thoughts and emotions. Quite a difference. The first holds our potential, the latter holds our stagnation."

"Could you explain the first part with a bit more detail?" Marsha asks.

"Sure. You are far, far more magnificent than you can imagine possible. Although most people never relate to themselves as magnificent, when a loving person is viewed from a metaphysical perspective, they are glorious. If they are angry, that changes, and they are a very much reduced and dimmer version. Because we are all Beings of energy, we are first and foremost metaphysical; only your physical body is three-dimensional. All your thoughts, emotions, feelings, imagination, intuition – everything that makes you, *you* – are on a fourth-dimensional level. Thus, you are multidimensional. As a Being of energy, you are immortal; you were not born, nor will you die. You are also a Being created from, and expressing, the Love and Light of divine creation.

"So, you are not a physical, mortal, body/personality with a soul, as you assume and live. You are a metaphysical, immortal soul with a mortal, and therefore temporary, body/personality. Completely the opposite of the way most people believe and live. That sums it up nicely!"

"My God . . . this is nothing like the interview that we came for," Peter mutters impatiently. "We need to get back on track."

I look at him sympathetically. "Yep . . . and right now you are so far off track into illusion it is too challenging to get back to the track of Truth. Right?"

"We didn't come here for this," he explodes.

I shake my head gently. "Actually, you did. If none of you came for this, it would not be happening. At the beginning of all this you told me that to a lesser degree you have the same problems as those people you help. That is what prompted this meeting. Tell me, will you not able to offer them more if you come from a position of Truth, rather than if you stand in the same deceitful illusions?"

Anita and Marsha share a long meaningful look. "We didn't know that we came for this, but we now see that we did," Anita says.

"Wonderful, but nevertheless, I do intend to back off somewhat."

"Speaking for myself, this is like manna from heaven," Bill says.

Smiling, Todd adds, "Not exactly the words I would use, but Bill speaks for me also."

Peter is now sitting, eyes downcast, as he sips a fresh mug of coffee. I realise that this is tough for him. I have witnessed this countless times in my Intensives as people struggle to fit my words into their old, outmoded beliefs. It is only when we are ready to release old concepts that we are able to move from the shadows into the Light. As a personality Peter is not ready, yet he is here, and this suggests that on a soul level, he is. For so many people this is the struggle; personality *versus* soul, instead of personality *with* soul. When we come together as a personality aiding and facilitating soul . . . in tandem, so to speak, we grow.

I explain this to them.

"Er . . . is there a single important key factor to our spiritual growth?" Anita asks, hesitantly.

I nod. "Another excellent question. There absolutely is, and that key factor is unconditional Love."

...FOUR...

Unconditional Love

Then said Almitra, 'Speak to us of Love.'
And he replied saying: *For even as Love crowns you,*
so shall he crucify you.
Even as he is for your growth, so he is for your pruning.
Even as he ascends to your height and caresses your
tenderest branches that quiver in the sun, so shall he
descend to your roots and shake them in their clinging
to the earth.

—Kahlil Gibran

"For a very long time, over a period of many centuries, we have created the idea and belief that Love is an emotion. It is not. Certainly we feel very strong high emotions when we experience Love, just as we feel very strong low emotions when we experience fear. But despite how they feel, these higher emotions are not Love."

"I don't quite get it. Can you explain further?" Marsha asks.

"If you were in an aeroplane and, after a long enjoyable period of stable flight it suddenly made strange noises, plunging toward the earth, you would be terrified. You would feel fear. What caused the fear? The plane

20

falling to Earth would cause you to create the emotions of fear. Right?"

"Of course," Marsha replies.

"And if you see your Mr. Perfect at a dance hall one Saturday night, and as you see him he sees you. Your eyes meet, your hearts flutter, and you are in Love. Suddenly, your emotions are at an all-time high. Right? But the emotions that result from this connection are not Love. Love is the *vehicle* of the emotions. Love created the emotions, but the emotions are not Love any more than the aeroplane is fear."

"So what is Love?" Anita asks.

"Ah . . . now we get to it. *Love is the power of creation.* Think about this for a moment. Love is the creative power of all life. Meaning, Love is the power that creates all life. God is Love. Yet, as we all know, God is not an emotion. The universe is created from Love, not from an emotion. We are Love. All humanity is Love . . . all Nature is Love.

"So here we have the paradox. We of humanity, created from Love, experience fear for most of our lifetimes . . . not Love. We abuse the very idea of Love. We have degraded the word Love to a sex act, to ownership, to a very low status, and we wonder why we struggle to stay alive. People say, 'I love my new car.' They do not, they covet it. People say, 'making love', when so often they are merely having sex; Love is not even involved. Love, as a word, has been hugely devalued in our casual relationship with ourselves and each other. And then we wonder why a long, lasting relationship based in a deep and abiding Love between two people is so rare, rather than so natural and common. We have reached the sad place where true Love is so devalued and so degraded that billions of people no longer experience it. We experience emotions that we *call* love, but mostly this is no more than deep emotional attachments. And, to be honest, most people do not want such knowledge. It is too confronting for them."

"How do you mean?" Marsha asks.

"There is a timing to Truth." I reply. "Truth out of timing is rejected. Jesus described it as 'casting pearls before swine'. How do you think people would feel if they were to fully realise that they had only experienced rare, fleeting moments of Love in their whole lives . . . if even that!"

"But they do experience Love," Marsha exclaims.

I sigh, not wanting to say this. "To experience Love you are required to be conscious. How do people experience Love when approximately ninety-four percent of humanity is living subconsciously for about ninety percent of every day, which is practically all of their lives?"

The three men and two women stare at me in shock.

A considerable silence follows.

"But...but this is not possible," Bill says. "Surely not," he adds pleadingly.

"I'm sorry, but we are a deluded, sick and sorry species," I tell them. "Just as we are also magnificent and creative Beings of the universe. Both are true . . . but we subconsciously live the first, and we have to consciously choose the latter. However, you may reject my words and we will agree to disagree."

"How can you reject words when they strike like arrows into your heart? How can you dismiss something that you have long suspected, just hoping that your own deeper thoughts were completely twisted and wrong?" says Bill heavily. "I wondered why I came along with the others when I knew that I had so much desk work, it didn't make sense. It does now."

I smile at them. "You are doing very well, you know. You all came breezing in here to simply discuss a few topics in life to assist with your work – and very commendably so, I might add – and you walk smack into me. Now, you are close to that place where life is never going to be the same again."

I chuckle. "It's like there is a bridge connecting two islands. One island is packed with bustling, busy people, while the other has very few people, yet the islands are connected by this bridge. It is not easy to see the bridge, however. To see it you have to open your inner eyes as well as your physical eyes, and not many people adjust to this, or are able to manage it. Many people vehemently deny the existence of such a bridge. However, if you have an open mind and an open heart, along with a developing sense of spiritual enquiry, you are able to discover the bridge and step onto it. And once you do so, there is no way back. There is nothing to prevent you from walking back to the crowded island, but it will not happen. Once you are on that bridge there is mostly a slow, stumbling walk across until you reach the other island. On arrival, you realise that everything is exactly the same, yet completely different. It's a freedom place. Well worth the struggle of the walk!"

"I'm still stunned and disconcerted by what you said about only being able to experience Love consciously," Bill says in a choking voice. "In the last few minutes I realise that I have only had those few fleeting moments of consciously experiencing Love. I experienced Love at the birth of each my three children, and I experienced Love as my wife was giving birth. All that terrible effort just blew me away and opened my heart to her. And yet . . . and yet . . ." he gives a great sigh, "I am aware that practically my whole life has been like a movie on a screen. A very familiar movie, but somehow removed from the vital moment of my life. I feel that I have been an onlooker from up here," he clutches his head, "instead of as a participant from in here," he thumps his heart dramatically. "And knowing all this hurts like hell," he ended, sobbing quietly into his hands.

Peter looks angry. "You see, I told you that we did not come here for this crap! Now look what's happened. We need to go."

Bill looks at him pityingly. "You just don't get it, do you? Here I am, having an inner revelation that will change my whole life into something far better – thanks to this enlightened man – and you get scared and angry." He smiles at Peter through moist eyes. "You're a good bloke, Pete. Just quit the anger and accept that you are here for an unexpected reason, just like all of us. When wisdom and insight are offered me, I'm just thankful that I have the sense to accept it, rather than react."

He looks at me. "I thank you most sincerely, sir."

I warmly smile at him. "You are very welcome.

"I'll continue on with this. What we experience and describe as Love is when our emotions are on a high. We will call this, human love. We have levels, or layers of emotions. The lower emotions are triggered by fears, by anger, criticism, and such like. If we are asked, 'Hi, how are you?' at this level, our reply is often, 'Not bad'. So we reply with a negative. When we rise up the scale of emotions to about halfway, life seems better, okay. To the question, 'Hi, how are you?' we are more likely to reply, 'Fine,' or 'Pretty good'. At the top of the scale, and we are feeling wonderful, then 'Great, thanks' is often the reply. All this is very normal and very human.

"However, our emotionally based human love is not divine Love, or absolute Love . . . or what I prefer to call, *unconditional* Love. It is mostly love *with* conditions. 'I love you darling, but . . . !' There can be quite a few buts in there. You understand my meaning?"

Four heads nod enthusiastically, one rather grudgingly.

"Okay. Now for the difficult part. You cannot Love another person before you *truly* Love yourself. When you unconditionally Love yourself, then you find that you are in Love with humanity. This does not mean that you approve of, or condone all human actions; it means that you Love the soul Beings they are. Unconditional Love is soul-based, not personality-based, although the personality can be included in this. This is why I Love humanity. I do not need to know a person to Love them, for we are *energetically* One. When you realise that there is nothing outside Self, then Self-Love becomes *All*-Love.

"And this, my friends, is why unconditional Love is so rare. We are not a species that easily Loves ourselves. We are a species that easily criticises and judges ourselves, thus we do the same for other people. All this is a very long haul from unconditional Love as a species."

"Wow," Anita says, her brown eyes looking sad. "So how do we learn to Love ourselves? Is it possible?"

"Do you see the irony of this?" I reply. "We *are* Love discovering Love through and within the individualisation of self. We are required to create Love to discover that we are, in fact, Love *creating* Love."

"Okay . . . bye-bye any clue as to what you are talking about," Todd says, with an easy smile. "I do know that it is profound and that it is imprinted in my heart, but I long for the moment when it makes full sense."

I smile. "And that, my friend, is the perfect attitude to adopt. If you do not destroy it by attempting to understand, that moment will surely arrive.

"We are a species at war with itself. Almost everyone lives with critical thoughts and feelings about themselves. Both physically and metaphysically, we are battlefields, each one of us. Is it any surprise that many nations are at war with other nations, or that political parties war with words against each other, when each person is doing this on an inner level all the time?"

"Do *you* do this?" Peter asks, an angry edge to his voice.

I expected this question would arise. "Actually, no, I do not. I never criticise myself, or judge myself. I never get angry with myself or other people. I have done that, but not for many years. I do not stress, nor do I get tired. I need sleep, and I enjoy plenty of it. I occasionally grumble, but quickly let it go. The same with reaction; it happens occasionally, but is quickly released. I do not worry, nor do I feel anxiety. All these negatives drain your vital energy, making you tired and exhausted. Neither do I experience fear in the way that I once did, nor do I conjure up the thoughts and emotions that create fear."

"How is it possible to live *like* that?" Bill asks.

I smile. "How is it possible to live *unlike* that? As a spiritual teacher, unconditional Love is the basis of what I teach in my Intensives. If people *live* what I teach, they are on the path from illusion to enlightenment. If they intellectualise what I teach, retaining it as unused knowledge, then not too much happens. It says in the Bible: the Truth shall set you free. A few essential words were missed out during one of the translations. If you *live* the Truth, the Truth will set you free. Very different. Not electronically store the knowledge, or covet the knowledge, or play clever with the knowledge, or write it on paper to keep such knowledge, but *live* it. Not so easy. Today, most people are addicted to knowledge and understanding. Both have problems attached."

Anita laughs. "So this brings us to knowledge and understanding."

I join with her laughter. "It does indeed. A natural progression."

...FIVE...

Knowledge and Understanding

And a man said, 'Speak to us of self-knowledge.'
And he answered saying: *Say not, "I have found the
truth," but rather "I have found a truth."*
Say not, "I have found the path of my soul."
Say rather, "I have met the soul walking on my path."
For the soul walks all paths.
*The soul walks not upon a line, neither does it grow
like a reed.*
The soul unfolds itself, like a lotus of countless petals.
—Kahlil Gibran

I SMILE AT ALL OF THEM. "Both knowledge and understanding are hugely overrated for our spiritual life, even though they play an important role in our daily life. We..."

Peter aggressively interrupts me. "How can you separate our daily life from our spiritual life?"

"If you were to listen, my friend, you will realise I am not stating a difference. As I was about to say, we live our daily life mostly with a physical focus, whereas we need to live our spiritual life with more of a metaphysical focus. I am sharing some of my spiritual knowledge with you, but this is not knowledge that is stored in my brain, just to trot out and use verbatim. This is what I call, *direct knowing*: it comes from the moment, from the heart/pineal/ whole-brain connection. The words may often be similar – after all, we only have twenty-six letters in our English alphabet – but the energy of each word flexes and changes with the energy of the moment. Thus, what I say is always fresh in energy, rather than stale and jaded.

"Not many people realise it, but some knowledge literally has a use-by date. Sure, there is knowledge that will stand the test of time, but there is also knowledge that will get stale and less pertinent as the months and years pass by. Knowledge that pertains to this moment is not necessarily the knowledge that will always be reliable. Energy changes, circumstances change, life changes, and people change."

"Give me an example of this," Peter demands.

I smile at him, not offended by his burgeoning fears and aggression.

"To do so will lead me into another area completely off-track with my current explanation. You have a choice. You can wait until our conversation brings that to the fore, or you can choose not to believe me. And in your anger, this will be far more to your liking, even if it is not to your advantage.

"To continue. The correct esoteric term for my *direct knowing* is mystical cognition. We are born with the ability to go way beyond our brain-knowledge and make intuitive leaps into direct knowing. Of course, this requires a high degree of self-trust, so it is not a common way for people to progress. We depend more on our brain power, on our knowledge, on our over-stimulated and often over-inflated intellects. Even our so-called knowledge is usually nothing more than information. Based in this, our knowledge is unformed and unrealised, changing as our information changes."

"You make it sound as if everything that could be wrong with us, is wrong," Peter declared. "So how come humanity is progressing so well?"

I laugh. "Progressing well! You see, that is *your* knowledge based in your unattainable wants, not knowledge based in reality. This is another of the problems with knowledge . . . it becomes personalised. Tell me, if we are progressing so well, how is it that around two-thirds of humanity lives at, or below, the poverty level? How is it that between thirty and forty thousand people, mostly Third World children, die of malnutrition and starvation every day? Why is suicide increasingly becoming an out-of-control problem in the Western World? You call this progressing well? Countries spend obscene amounts of money on weapons to kill, simply because fear and control are dominant in the lives of the nations' leaders. How clever is that? You are living in a delusion. Right now, Peter, you are lashing out at me because I am showing you the falsities of your own life. But, you also unwittingly revealed another flaw in knowledge. There is knowledge based in facts, and knowledge based in fiction. Who determines which is which? So much 'common knowledge' is make-believe, rumour, deliberately misleading misinformation, and sheer wishful thinking."

My voice becomes more powerful as my energy rises.

"And this brings us to self-knowledge. Our knowledge of self is seriously flawed. We think of ourselves as physical and mortal, with death awaiting at the end of our lives. Wrong! As I have already stated, we are metaphysical and immortal, living timelessly. Deluded suicide victims return to a similar scenario each time they incarnate. Death is the illusion. Knowledge of the illusion in which people live is *not* knowledge based in Truth. Such knowledge leads to despair and anxiety, to disease and suicide. Please don't talk to me about humanity progressing well. Like a fish out of water, we are gasping and choking on the malignant and destructive illusions contained within our own so-called knowledge."

"Please, sir, don't be too annoyed with Pete. Like a panicky swimmer, he is way out of his depth. He's a good person," Bill says, with sincerity.

"Actually, I'm not annoyed. Not in the least, but I'm a passionate man and when my energy rises my voice rises with it. Peter triggered words that might never have been spoken, but they needed saying. It's all perfect."

Anita gives me a serious look. "When you come on strong like that, it makes me tremble, yet it has nothing to do with fear."

I chuckle. "The soul you are is getting excited. Truth is rather like soul food, so I suspect that the tremble comes from deep within. If you are open and receptive today, perhaps you might enjoy a soul feast."

I smile at the group, including Peter. I feel for him. "If you are ready, we have briefly looked at knowledge, now I'll put 'understanding' under the spotlight. We are raised at school to learn our lessons, to learn how to read, to spell, to write, also mathematics and many other intellectual abilities we need in daily life. All good. Nevertheless, during this educative process we develop a strong need to understand. In fact, because of the way we are so often judged and graded while at school, many people develop a deep subconscious fear of *not* understanding!

"Not for a moment am I denying understanding its appropriate place in life. Understanding and the intellect rightfully go hand-in-hand. However, the direct knowing I mentioned, the mystical cognition or intuitive leaps, whatever, is not based in understanding. Understanding is basically a left-brain function, while direct knowing is basically right-brain. If we all had the ability to use our whole-brain at will, we could both understand *and* make the intuitive leaps. This happens, but it is rare. It is considered that approximately eighty percent of the human population is now left-brain dominant. Not good. People like me who are born right-brain dominant are the minority. This is not *better,* but it does make other brain skills more available."

"Such as?" Anita asks, visibly more relaxed.

"You are not going to like this. The left-brain's primary function is about survival, competition, logic, and practicality. To experience direct knowing we are required to trust – it is an essential component – but the left-brain is unable to trust. Trust is not a left-brain function, it is whole-brain and/ or right-brain function. To understand something, we draw on knowledge from the past, so understanding is always based in the past, never in the moment. This is a problem because life is based in the moment and never in the past!"

"Oh God," Anita groans dramatically, "you're doing it again. Just as I begin to get a handle on something you say, you twist it away from me."

"You see, once again this is your need to understand. *Listen carefully.* Truth is always in the moment, it never leaves it. So to walk a spiritual path of Truth is to walk in ever unfolding Mystery – with a capital M. Obviously, you cannot *understand* this very real, yet mystical Mystery. Understanding takes you into the past, while Mystery is creative energy in the eternal moment. Most people chose the illusions of understanding. I chose eternal Mystery . . . the place of *knowing,* rather than knowledge."

"I find the whole concept of knowledge having a use-by date – as you mentioned earlier – very challenging. Would you be kind enough give us an example of this?" Bill asks.

I chuckle. "I knew this would come around. This will also answer your earlier demand, Peter. Remember, you asked for this. Let's see if it is a Truth out of timing for you. Okay, in the time of Christ there was much mention made of forgiveness. This has persisted, and today we are told that we must practice forgiveness. This is outdated knowledge that was never based in Truth. I'll tell you a principle of human Truth: *In every moment of your life, you are creating the direction and the content of every moment of your life.* In effect, this means that you are the sole creator of your life. Nobody else, just you. This also means that nobody else ever did anything to you that was not part of your soul creation, because we are talking about soul-level creation here.

"To forgive other people for what they have done to you is pure illusion, simply because *you are the creator of your life.* All forgiveness is based in blame. You blame a person, you forgive that person. Blame and forgiveness hold hands. While you have one you will always have the other. When you let go of blame, you no longer need to forgive. And this includes yourself."

Bill shakes his head. "So much, so deep, so connected."

I nod. "The people who you blame and forgive had to collaborate with you on a soul level to meet your karmic needs. Remember, your life is not a born, live, die, affair. Your life is all eternity, endlessly incarnating in one, ever growing continuity of Self."

"So why would Christ say something that was wrong?" Marsha asks.

"Not wrong, incorrect. Why? Because in his wisdom he spoke to the people at their level of . . . dare I say it . . . understanding. Truth out of timing does not bear fruit! We play the same game today, except the religions and people that preach this do not have the insights of a greater wisdom. This is a perfect example of the use-by date of knowledge. Hearing of this example, an enlightened person would smile, and say, 'He spoke with the words that were appropriate,' while an unenlightened person would be challenged, arguing about what they do not understand and cannot explain."

"So if someone ran their car into my car while I am stopped at a traffic light, for example, you are saying that I created this?" Marsha asks.

"I'm saying that you are an unwitting co-creator. We like to call this an accident, but an accident implies that everything is separate and random, and can therefore collide. This is false. Everything is within One field of energy, thus nothing is random and nothing can *accidentally* collide. Cars *can* collide, but never by accident. The drivers have a soul agenda that they consciously know nothing about. Neither does the law or the courts have a clue about Oneness. And so we muddle along, lost in the illusion."

"If or when we sue the offender and take them to court for damages," Marsha continues, "what does this create?"

"It creates a deepening discord between the two drivers who will, all unknowingly, continue the contest either in the same incarnation, or in the next . . . until eventually the discord is brought to a peaceful conclusion."

"And we never know this is happening!" Marsha says incredulously.

"Of course not. If you did know you would accept full responsibility for every aspect of your life, knowing there is no such thing as an accident. As a result, your whole life would change dramatically."

"How? Why?"

"Because you would be aware that you are the creator of all that takes place and happens in your life. You would *live and act consciously,* rather than live and react subconsciously. You would live with actions in the moment, rather than with reactions from the past. This would change everything. It is so simple . . . and obvious!"

Marsha surges to her feet and strongly embraces me. "You have shown me something that is going to change my life. It's as though I have been fumbling in the dark forever and you have just switched on the light. Thank you so much." Tears of gratitude trickle from her eyes, as she blinks at me with a happy, but bemused expression. "Wow!"

"My pleasure, truly. I just love it when Truth connects. You are right, it literally switches on a light. But it is Truth that does this, not me."

"Anyway . . . . I suggest that it's time to stretch our legs and take a walk in the garden."

So saying I get up, encouraging everyone to do the same. "Come on, let's blow away some of the cobwebs of illusion. A bit of fresh air is always appropriate."

. . . SIX . . .

The Power of Trust

Trust is always unconditional, or it is not trust: it is hope in disguise. The power of trust creates a life that responds to the creative power of trust. Trust changes the way I experience life. Because I trust myself unconditionally, my experience carries the result of this trust into my daily life. We are each the creators of our own lives. When you add the element of trust, the illusions melt away and a greater reality comes forth.

—Michael J. Roads

CLOSELY FOLLOWED BY ANITA, I walk out through the glass sliding doors and onto the verandah. She immediately notices our swimming pool, converted years ago into a pond.

"Oh wow! I love it. Full of life and perfectly natural."

While her words might not be fully accurate – a converted swimming pool is hardly natural – it does carry its own charm. The large floating island I created in the middle of the pool from poly-downpipes and polystyrene fruit boxes, long ago became host to some luxuriant ferns and a mass of plants that completely covered and swamped the whole caboodle. It *does* look natural, very lush and green, and rather tropical. It is home to a whole host of frogs, hunting snakes – hopefully not too many – and the aforementioned water dragons. Add to this the bromeliads and other plants masking the pool edge, and the overall effect *is* rather striking.

The others are now clustered together, all looking at the island.

"On one level you are looking at a reality covering a lesser illusion."

"How do you mean?" Bill asks.

"Well under the reality of lush and prolific vegetation is the stark, white plastic and poly foundations on which it all floats. It's not a good example of illusion and reality, but a spiritual teacher has to use whatever is at hand," I say with a broad smile. "And meanwhile the wildlife could not care less."

"Wildlife?" asks Anita.

I nod. "Yes, quite a few frog species, the occasional, temporary, hunting tree snake, a number of water dragons, and who knows what other tiny creatures. It has become very naturalised, especially when you realise that I did not plant any of those ferns. They all came from spores."

"Where . . . ?" began Anita.

"Did the spores come from? I have no idea. Just blew in, I guess. But the nice part is they are the perfect ferns for the job," I reply. "This is how Nature works. If you have an invasion of weeds on farmland or in a garden and, as is common, they are predominantly a single species of weeds, you will find that the soil, if tested, will have a mineral or trace element deficiency. In the way of Nature, the weed invasion will be high in that deficient element, thus transferring it into the soil via its roots. Daisies are high in calcium, thus you find masses of them in lawns growing on acidic soil."

"Huh . . . more than just a spiritual teacher," Todd laughs. "But I happen to know that you are a keen and knowledgeable organic gardener."

I smile at them, careful to include Peter. "I sometimes wonder whether I am a spiritual teacher who is a gardener, or a gardener who is a spiritual teacher," I say, laughing. "But the gardener came first, so I guess this is the way of it."

"When did you begin gardening," Anita asks.

"When I was six. My dad gave me six tomato plants. We set his six and mine at the same time. A month later his six were growing well, while mine were languishing; alive but not growing. When I tearfully pointed this out to him, he was baffled by it. 'I dig mine out every afternoon to see if the roots are growing,' I sobbed, 'and they never are.'

"That was when I learned about trusting what you cannot see, because obviously we cannot see roots underground. And I remember later, when dad's tomatoes were finished, mine came into full fruit. I was hooked. All those amazing and delicious tomatoes from such ordinary little plants."

"You're a wise man," Bill said. "I easily see the correlation of trusting that the roots are growing underground, and thereby trusting all the unseen and unseeable elements in our life."

I nod. "What very few people realise is that we are the creators of our lives. Every tiny detail, from our murders, our accidents, our muggings, our misfortune or fortune, our wealth or poverty, illness or good health . . . all of it. Inadvertently, we create it all in the ongoing saga of our lives. While we remain in the illusion, believing that life is as we see it through our physical eyes, and experience through our physical senses, then it will continue to appear as fortune or misfortune, accidents and folly, etc., etc. If however, we were to introduce Truth, based on a greater reality, into our lives, rather than manipulating the illusion, our lives would go through a gradual, or even rapid change, depending on our openness."

"So you are saying that trust is an element which is based in Truth?" Todd asks.

"I am indeed. When you trust yourself, everything changes."

"But heaps of people trust themselves," Anita objects.

"Actually, no. The numbers of people who fully trust themselves are very thin on this planet." I smile benignly. "There is more to this."

"Of course there is, "Anita says, with a laugh. "You are going to turn me upside down again. Okay . . . I'm ready and holding on!"

"Consider our insurance system. Is this based in trust . . . or fear?"

Todd laughs. "Okay, I'll bite. Obviously, it is totally fear based."

"Correct. Listen carefully. You cannot have fear and trust in the same state of consciousness. I told you earlier that I do not experience worry or anxiety. How could I possibly trust *and* experience worry and anxiety?"

"I suppose you couldn't," Anita suggests, shrewdly.

"Exactly right. I trust unconditionally. And I know that trust is one of the great powers of creation. Trust is always unconditional, or it is not trust: it is hope in disguise. The power of my trust creates a life that responds to the creative power of trust. So trust changes the way I experience life. Because I unconditionally trust, my experience carries the result of the trust that I have into my life. Do you get it? We are the creators of our lives. So add the element of trust, and illusions melt away and a greater reality comes forth."

"Oh God . . . you did it again. And I was hanging on," Anita sighs. "But what is it that you trust? Do you trust life? Or God? Or what?"

"Another good question. I trust Self. I trust self as a person, and Self as an immortal Being of Love and Light."

"And this changes everything?" Todd asks, bewildered. "How can trust change life? Life does things to us. It messes us around."

"No. Life does not mess us around. We unknowingly do this in the illusion. Our every action has a reaction. When you are unaware of the actions, then the reactions are experienced as life messing us around. Add to this, most of our actions are actually reactions. By this I mean we are reacting to reactions without ever realising it. *This* messes us around!"

"I just don't get it," Bill says.

"Okay, if you don't get it, I need to explain a bit further. I did not want to go too deep . . . but, no choice. In the illusion, you see life as an outside Self event. It is not. In a greater reality, life is an inside Self event. When you realise that *you* are life, that *you* are the world, then you realise that there is nothing outside Self. When you realise this, when you *know* this as a living reality, you become aware of your own powers of creation. You add trust to the amalgam we call life and you change it. This is spiritual alchemy.

"Remember how I said that all life is *One* energy? You *are* that energy. All life is you. You are all life. Thus, you are the creator of your life. Yes?"

"Sorry," Anita said, "but I am upside down sitting on my pickled brains. So, no, I don't get it . . . but in my heart, I feel it. Does that make sense?"

"Actually, feeling it is far better. You asked if I trust life, God, or what. I trust Self. I am life, I am God, just as each of us is; every human Being, so with the trust which I create, I change the creation of my life. The past, the present and the future. Surely you can grasp this."

"You just said that you create this trust. Don't we all have trust and just use it to different varying degrees, some more or less than others?" Anita replies. "This is a fundamental belief."

"No, it does not work like that. We are here to learn creation, so there are no freebies, no hand-outs. If we want to trust, we create trust."

"Well I was always taught that we have to learn to trust. This implies that we already have it, but have to learn to use it," Peter says, hostilely.

"Of course you were," I reply. "So was I. But they were wrong. How can anyone who has never experienced trust, teach what trust is? I learned to *create* trust, so now I trust."

"So how do I create trust?" Marsha asks, quietly.

I sigh. "This sounds so simple, and it is simple, but so very difficult to do. You make a decision to trust yourself unconditionally and that you will keep on trusting yourself, no matter what. The reality is you will betray your trust over and over, day after day, but you need to *keep on* consciously trusting yourself. For example, you promise yourself that you will focus on trust ten times in the morning and the same in the afternoon . . . but after just three times in the morning, you forgot for the rest of the day. Next day you simply continue doing the best you can. You promised yourself that today you would begin to take better care of your health, starting with eliminating sugary drinks, yet you drank them just the same. Tomorrow you trust yourself again, pursuing the same goal. Unconditional trust. One day, it will change.

"You have to let go of needing an acceptable outcome, or of any expectations of how long this will take. You trust yourself without any conditions, hour by hour, day by day, week by week, month by month, year by year. You simply continue to consciously keep on trusting Self/ self. I'll explain a bit more about trust and creation. Remembering what I told you about the One energy of humanity, nevertheless every person is an individual field-of-energy. It's a complete paradox: individualising Oneness! And, for the umpteenth time, where you focus, your energy flows . . . and *creates*. As many times a day as you can – maybe thirty times – you focus on unconditionally trusting yourself, forming the trust thoughts in your self-talk, and feeling the uplifting emotions of yourself creating inner trust. Elation, joy, accomplishment, confidence, these are the emotions you create and feel. As you do this you are creating within your personal field-of-energy. Gradually, you are stitching – not the right word but it creates the right picture – new energy into your own personal field-of-energy, and this new energy is trust. You are the creator of your self and your life. Gradually, over a period of time this new energy that you have created has an increasing influence on you, until the moment comes that your self-created trust overwhelms you . . . and Trust in Self is real. You now trust, and your life completely changes."

"And how long will all this take?" Peter asks, sceptically.

"You just don't get it, do you?" I reply. "I suggest that you prise open that steel-jawed trap that you call a mind and cut yourself a bit of slack. I am not opposing you, you are opposing yourself. You are your own opposition. Let me assure you, Peter, that opposing yourself does not work. In this way you are creating an unhappy life."

"You know nothing about me," Peter snaps angrily.

"Actually, just listening to you and watching your rigid body language, you would be surprised by how much I have already learned about you. Like it or not, your energy communicates."

I hold up my hands toward him in a gesture of peace. "Consider this. You are my guest. I did not invite you here; I accepted your group request. So please do me the curtesy of either listening, or remove yourself. I am not here to convince you of anything. You may believe or disbelieve whatever you like. It makes no difference to me. Those are your options."

Todd and Bill both move toward Peter and walk him a distance away, where they all go into a verbal huddle.

"Sorry about this," Anita says.

"Yeah, me to," from Marsha. "Peter is the classic cynic. We thought he might be good to bring along, in case we were all too gullible. Now we can see just how stupid our thinking was. We literally had no idea of what we were about to engage in. It never occurred to us that we might become fully involved, or that being with you, listening to your words, and even being in your energy could be a life-changing experience."

Marsha shakes her head. "God . . . how stupid can you get?"

I laugh. "Not stupid at all. Seriously, how often have you ever been exposed to Truth, spoken to you by a person who experiences it?"

She shakes her head even more vigorously. "Like . . . never!"

...SEVEN...

Giving and Receiving

Then said a rich man, 'Speak to us of giving.'
And he answered saying: *There are those who give*
and know not the pain in giving, nor do they seek joy,
nor give with the mindfulness of virtue; they give as
in the yonder valley the myrtle breathes its fragrance
into space.
Through the hands of such as these God speaks,
and from behind their eyes He smiles upon the earth.

—Kahlil Gibran

I CHUCKLE. "SO WHAT DID YOU EXPECT? A lecture from a little old man, who hopefully could teach you what you wanted to know and nothing else?"

Anita laughs loudly. "Something like that. And you are not little, or old . . . or at least, you don't look it. You're a powerhouse! You're nothing like we expected. And we expected nothing like we've received."

"Hmm, an interesting subject to talk about; giving and receiving," I reply.

"I can't see why. Giving and receiving is about as ordinary an everyday affair as anything can be," Anita says.

I nod. "It would certainly seem that way, but not all is exactly as it seems."

"You have made that very clear," Anita replies, ruefully. "So let's hear about the hidden reality of giving and receiving."

"There is nothing hidden, Anita, I simply said that all is not quite as it seems."

Noticing that the three men have joined us again and are listening, I move my eyes to each person in turn, engaging them. "I am going to ask you all a question. Be totally honest in your answer. Put your hands up those of you who can easily give."

Almost immediately, five hands went into the air. No hesitation.

I smile all around. "This is as I expected. Now, being fully as honest, put your hands up those of you who can *just as easily* receive."

Two hands went up immediately, only to come halfway down as the question fully percolated. Two other hands made it halfway, then hesitated, wavering uncertainly. Todd's hand went up slowly, and steadily remained.

"Thank you for being honest. Only one of you can receive as easily as he can give. The others are unsure enough to state clearly that no, you are not able to receive as easily as you can give. This is normal. If I ask this question at an Intensive, apart from a very few, almost everyone can easily give. But when it comes to receiving, only about a quarter of them find it easy. For the others it is more difficult. The question is . . . why?"

I wait as they look to me for the answer. When they realise they are expected to respond, they look a mite worried.

"Well, as dumb as it sounds, I guess receiving makes me feel more beholden to someone, like I owe them," Anita says.

I continue waiting.

"Okay, from my angle receiving makes you feel *lesser*, while giving allows you to feel *greater*," Bill offers.

I nod. "Both very pertinent. Any more?"

Marsha nods. "I agree. Receiving seems to reduce my sense of self-worth, while giving seems to increase it."

Todd smiles easily. "I guess I see it differently. When I was a kid it was all receive, and I didn't feel lesser, or reduced . . . just grateful. It has stayed that way all along."

Peter is silent, offering nothing.

I smile at them. "There are no rights or wrongs to any of this, but you have said it well. The average person who struggles to receive will often grumble about not liking charity, but the truth is mostly about their loss of self-worth, self-esteem. And from a common viewpoint, understandable."

"Okay," says Anita, with an impish grin, "turn it upside down."

"What is seldom ever considered is that in giving and receiving there is very little difference. The receiver gives the giver the gift of giving, while the giver is able to give to the receiver. Each is a giver, each is a receiver in the very same act."

Anita cocks her head sideways at me. "Well, you did it again. That's a very different way of looking at it . . . and one that cannot be disputed."

I smile at her. She really has an engaging personality.

"People give for many different reasons. Oftentimes it is because the giver can easily afford to give and it gives them an inner pleasure. And this is okay. Some give to be known as generous and kindhearted, for their inner thoughts of themselves are unkind. And this is okay. Some give that they should be *seen* to give, while others give anonymously, hiding their gifting. All this is okay. Some who live on the edge of poverty, and cannot afford to give anything at all, willingly give of all that they have to share with their fellows. There are so many forms of giving, but always there is an unseen energetic connection between the giver and receiver, and only on this soul level is the full truth of giving and receiving fully recognised and acknowledged. And it is all okay."

Todd lets out a deep breath. "I like your explanation. But how about begging? When I am overseas I never know how to deal with this. And now daily on Internet there are so many good causes all wanting money to support them. In a way, this is a modern form of begging, even if it is always for a good cause. And then there is phone begging for a cause. I cannot give to them all, yet I feel guilty when I don't, even though I cannot possibly afford to."

I nod sympathetically. "I know exactly what you mean. There is no should or shouldn't answer, there is only dealing with it in the best way that you can."

"So how do *you* deal with it?" Todd asks. "You travel a lot and you have an Internet presence, so you obviously get subjected to all this."

"Indeed I do. I follow my heart within the dictates of my finances. In an Austrian city a few years ago, from a restaurant I watched a man with badly deformed legs walk a tortured twenty metres before he sank to the pavement, his hat in front of him, his eyes downcast. In that moment, his plight touched my heart. When I went out and passed him by, I dropped a twenty euro note in his hat. He looked both startled and deeply grateful. To those who touch me in the moment, I give generously. If this does not happen, I pass them by.

"As for Internet, I have those to whom I give, along with a few charities, the rest I leave. Only a very wealthy man can give to all of them. I am not a wealthy man, although I am a very rich one."

Marsha frowns at me. "How do you mean? What's the difference?"

"Wealth is money stored above and beyond your needs. Fear needs to be made secure with wealth, although it never is! Rich, for me, means that I have abundance in all aspects of my life; in my relationships, my health, and my mental and emotional status. On a soul level all the riches, wisdom, intelligence and diversity of my spiritual life remains with me forever. That, my friends, is my definition of *truly* being rich."

Bill nods knowingly. "Nobody can argue with that."

Marsha sighs. "While all our material wealth is left behind! And we spend all our lives working for this. It doesn't make much sense, does it?"

"This is why, at around thirty-five years of age, I decided to follow my path of spiritual inquiry. Now, my lifetime accumulation of wisdom and mastery is always fresh, in the moment, and available forever. It does not need a physical body to access it, nor is it locked away like money in a bank account. It is now fundamental to who I am."

"Why didn't they teach this stuff at school?" Anita sighs.

"First, the school teachers know nothing of this, and even if they did the kids would not listen to it. Everything comes in timing."

... EIGHT ...

Timing, Time and Timelessness

And an astronomer said, 'Master, what of time?' And he
answered: *You would measure time, the measureless
and the immeasurable. You would adjust your conduct and
even direct the course of your spirit according to hours and
seasons. Of time you would make a stream upon whose
bank you would sit and watch its flowing.*
*Yet the timeless in you is aware of life's timelessness, and
knows that yesterday is but today's memory and tomorrow
is today's dream.*

—Kahlil Gibran

"THERE WE ARE, another brilliant topic!"

"What is?"

"Timing. It's time we broached the subject of time, timing, and even of timelessness."

"This sounds weird," Anita chuckles.

I realise it is also time for me to move the people away from a cluster by the pond and out into the garden.

"Come along, folks. Follow me down the steps and into the garden.

Who knows, fresh new outer views may stimulate fresh new inner views!"

They follow me down the sixteen wood steps and on past our patio. I have no intention of keeping them in the garden for long, but they need a bit of fresh air and a stretch. I sigh. As I suspected, it's going to be a long day.

We go down a few more rock steps, stopping by the lily pond, where a number of large, colourful, tropical waterlilies grow.

"This is one example of time and timing right here. We measure time with a clock, but the waterlilies measure time only by the seasons. All Nature is this way . . . except us. Yet even we have to bow to the seasons and the weather when it disrupts our orderly timetables."

"How do you mean?" Marsha asks.

I smile. "It is common in many airports around the world to have all air traffic come to a standstill. Summer storms in America, dense winter fog in England, snow and ice in Northern Europe, that sort of thing. All our nicely calculated time schedules are thrown into complete disarray."

I watch as they all nod knowingly. We have all experienced that notably unpleasant inconvenience.

I point into the water. "In this pond there are the larvae of dragonflies. They live in the water for months or years, depending on the variety, until in perfect timing they emerge from the water, climbing up the lily stalks to go through the transformation from a water-going predator to an aerial predator. And always in perfect timing, even though they know nothing of time.

"The waterlilies are almost, not quite, dormant in our subtropical winter, but as the water warms, so the timing for their vigorous growth and flowering is triggered. Everything in Nature has a timing, and Nature is acutely aware of this timing, very rarely violating it. To a degree, we also live within Nature's timing, especially the seasonal timing, but we also live within a vast, universal timing of which we seem to be completely unaware."

I pause, waiting for the inevitable question. It comes on cue!

"What universal timing? I've never heard of such a thing." says Bill.

I smile. "Okay . . . this again opens up Pandora's Box. I'll lift the lid gently, so as not to disturb too many of the contents. We are universal Beings living in a form of denial. Generally speaking, our focus is so material and physical that we have little awareness of our universal nature. Speaking for myself, I am aware of a vast cosmic timetable. Whereas there is no set or fixed timing, there *are* huge cycles of timing in which we have the opportunity to spiritually grow and develop. These take place over hundreds of millennia, during which time we have thousands of incarnations. As I hinted at earlier, we are now living at the end of one of those huge cycles. The one that is . . ."

"How long a cycle?" Bill cuts in.

I sigh, giving him an exasperated smile. "As I was about to say, the one that is currently ending is approximately a two hundred thousand year cycle. Please don't get overly attached to the linear timing. The universe runs to its own particular rhythm, rather than our perception of linear time. During this cycle the majority of incarnating people have been locked into a stagnating, subconscious pattern of sameness, and thus have not been growing in consciousness. Oh sure, we have experienced a great intellectual development during this time, but we have not grown in either wisdom or intelligence. We are a fearful species, not a wise one. Our cleverness has far outstripped our wisdom. And clever, as is very evident, holds hands with stupid!"

"So what does this all mean in terms of our lives and living them?" Bill asks, looking slightly disturbed.

"It means that as immortal Beings who continue to incarnate, we are at a time when the majority will incarnate into another repeat pattern of the past, while the few will move on into incarnations of new experiences. Let me state, however, that the majority will have exactly the same opportunities to spiritually grow as have always been available. *We* are the creators of our lives . . . and nothing changes this."

"I find this disturbing," Bills says. "It's like a judgement."

"Why?" I ask. "If you are in grade four at school and you fool around instead of applying yourself to your lessons, then it is common that you have to repeat grade four the following year, instead of going up to fifth grade with the rest of the class. However, in this universal grading, it is practically the whole class that has to repeat the grade, while only a very few go up a higher grade. It is not a matter of being superior or more clever; it is all about applying ourselves to the Truth of who we are as eternal universal

Beings, as opposed to the belief that we are a mortal and short-term species who are successful only if we accumulate a big hoard of money.

"How stupid is that?" I chuckle. "To get caught in cycles of making money to simply leave it behind, so the only things that go with you are the endless beliefs that tether you to sameness."

"And this fits in with timing, *how*?" Peter asks, icily.

"Another good question. In Nature the timing of a bud unfolding into a flower is usually determined by the warmth of the sun and the moisture from the rain. Imagine a person taking a bud and tearing the petals open! You would not get a beautiful open flower, you would have a destroyed flower. Why? It was out of timing for the bud. Everything has its timing. An egg hatches after a certain period of incubation. Ice and snow and frost, along with sun and rain are all an integral aspect of timing in Nature. For us, however, *we* are the timing of our own growth. *We* determine when, or if, we will grow. The universe prompts all of us, but only a minority is listening. A few people attempt to trigger their timing with drugs. Oftentimes they are seeking a spiritual Truth, yet it is not their timing, so they resort to drugs . . . and it doesn't work. No matter how high they get, they come back to a lower place than from where they started. For us, the time of the timing is created by being *aware*, by being *conscious*, not by force.

"And the people who inner-work to create – or co-operate with – such timing are often considered to be crackpots! You are talking with one. So many of my friends from the past thought I was crazy-weird, scarcely bothering to earn money, while doggedly and enthusiastically pursing my spiritual quest."

A long, thoughtful silence follows.

"The problem with listening to you is that as disturbing as it is, all you say makes perfect sense. It's as though you are giving me the answers to questions that I have not yet thought of, yet they exist in some deep inner place. That alone is disturbing." Bill says, into the silence.

I put a hand on his shoulder and gently squeeze. "My friend, I am glad that you are disturbed. When a person sleeps, the only way out of that sleep is to disturb them. This creates the opportunity to wake up."

I laugh. "This is what I do. I disturb sleepy people and help them to

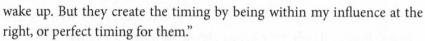

wake up. But they create the timing by being within my influence at the right, or perfect timing for them."

Bill looks me in the eyes. "I admit, I came here with a sleepy interest. Now, my world will never be the same again. This disturbs me. Will my marriage survive this? I don't know. Maybe Mary is ready for a new me, I can only hope and pray that she is, because you have lit a fuse that will never go out. And honestly, I'm afraid of the inevitable explosion!"

I smile at him sympathetically. "You'll be okay, trust me on this. You are level-headed and sincere, you'll be okay. Bring Mary along to my next Intensive so you are able to grow together. Togetherness is a great marriage. And please, don't think that I'm soliciting for participants. I don't do that. If it is the right timing for you, as it obviously is, the chances are good that it will be in right timing for Mary."

"And if it isn't?"

"Bill, where you focus, your energy flows. Rather than focus on the negative possibilities, I suggest you focus on the positive ones. Life unfolds in a far more pleasant way when you do this. It's all part of our creation, not luck or chance, or anything outside of ourselves."

"You see, that's what I mean. You see life as our creation, within us, while to the rest of the world it is the reverse of this. It's like you are asking us to throw away lifetimes of beliefs that everyone agrees with, simply because you say that they are wrong," Marsha verbally explodes.

I shake my head. "People, be fair. Have I asked any of you to believe me? I think not. You are welcome to all your beliefs. But please, do me a favour. Ask yourselves if those beliefs created *truly* happy lives for your grandparents, or your parents? Have they lived uplifting and self-honouring lives? If they have, then I suggest that we end this and you follow those old beliefs and concepts that worked so well for them."

Peter smiles grimly. "You know damn well, they haven't. I can't speak for all of us, but I dare bet that to some degree we all have messed up grandparents and parents. I certainly have. This is what frightens me. A . . . life of misery like my father. Only to end in a hospital bed with cancer. Scary. Geez . . . no thank you."

He looks at me grimly. "Tell me honestly, is this what illusions do for people? Can you teach me how to live in a way that avoids all this?"

"I don't teach people how to avoid anything. I teach people how to fully engage life by following the principles of Truth. They work beneficially *for* us. But what people do with what I teach is entirely their own responsibility. Illusions are unable to fully support life, because they hold no true energy. Illusions are like candles in the dark; they hold the darkness of our fears away for a little while, but eventually they flicker, and burn out. Then the darkness of our fears is back, and we realise that the fears never really went away."

"Within this group, Peter, you are the one who is closest to the dynamic of actual change. My words are igniting you; this is why you are so reactive. My words terrify you, because you are experiencing the collapse of the whole hollow structure of your life. And this is understandable, because it is all you had. I sympathise with you, but I am also excited for you. You, my friend, came here in perfect timing."

He laughs harshly. "Yeah . . . ironic, isn't it? Who would have thought that mere words could hold such power?"

... NINE ...

The Power of Words

My words hold Truth, which in the moment of your
perfect timing become powerful, life changing. If the
same words are spoken out of your timing, they are
without power, and easily dismissed.
                                        —Michael J. Roads

"THERE ARE WORDS, MY FRIEND, and then there are words, for not all words are equal. Even identical words hold different energies according to the speaker. My words hold Truth, which in your moment of timing, become powerful. If the same words were out of your timing, they would be easily dismissed."

" . . . as I have tried to dismiss yours. Trouble is, they won't stay dismissed," Peter says, with a frown. "And . . . maybe this is a good thing."

"Why is this?" Anita asks. "I mean, why or how can power be placed into words. After all is said and done, words are nothing more than just words."

I smile at her. "If you believe that, then how do you rationalise some of the great speeches of the world? And there are many examples. Take Martin Luther King, Jr, when he spoke to the crowds with his famous 'I have a dream . . . ' speech, outlining his great vision. Electrifying. And John F. Kennedy; 'Ask not what your country can do for you, but what you can do for your country.' There are many examples from great men and women throughout the ages. And it is not as though each speech was based in Truth. It was based in passion and a powerful inner conviction. Words are not merely sounds. Words carry the energy of the speaker. And this can be for better or worse. Hitler used the power of words to draw out the latent self-righteousness and hate within many of the people of his nation in his time. I emphasise, he drew out the hate; he could not create it within other people."

"Obviously I hadn't thought this one through," Anita comments, wryly. "But I still think there is more to this that you have not yet mentioned."

Nodding, I say, "True, of course, but it opens up another can of worms."

Anita laughs. "That's okay. We can tip the can of worms into Pandora's Box and they can all wriggle around together. Should be fun."

I laugh. "Okay, you win. As energetic Beings we have chakras with both our physical body and our metaphysical body. These chakras are our energy centres, for as I have said, we are Beings of pure energy. There are seven main chakras with the physical body, and five with the metaphysical body. To metaphysical vision, a chakra appears as a vertical spinning wheel of energy. Each is a different colour and each has a different energy value. In spiritual literature this is all well-known and very well documented.

"Briefly . . . the seven chakras of the physical body are the Base Chakra, which is red, near our tailbone; the Sacral Chakra, orange, near our sexual area; the Solar Plexus Chakra, yellow, just above the navel; the Heart Chakra, green, over the heart; the Throat Chakra, blue, over the Adam's apple; the Brow Chakra, indigo, in the centre of the brow; and finally the Crown Chakra, violet, literally on the crown of the head. This will do for my explanation. From red base up, they have an ascending scale in energy, higher and finer. Okay?" They all nod. Todd, Anita and Marsha indicate that they are reasonably familiar with this. Peter and Bill look a bit blank.

"These chakras are either open and active or closed and inactive. This all depends on us. All twelve of my chakras are open and active. This is not common. The Throat Chakra is the chakra of communication . . . and herein lies the power of words. If this chakra is closed, as is quite common, then you will not be stirred by such a person's words. Some university lecturers have a closed throat chakra. They are bored by their subject and disconnected from their students. With these people you will need to take copious notes, for you will have difficulty remembering what they say.

"On the other end of the scale are the university lecturers who have a passion for their subject and delight in their students. Their throat charka will be open and their words will almost burn into the listeners, igniting them to learn more. And some of their key phrases will be remembered for many years. So you see, the power of words varies not with the words, but with the speaker of the words."

Anita nods sagely. "Okay, I get it. This makes sense. It reminds me of the late Steve Irwin, the crocodile hunter. He had passion, oodles of it, and his words penetrated into me like lasers beams."

"Exactly right. It was not the content of his words that took much of the world by storm, it was the heartfelt passion *within* his words that ignited people. His words connected his passion with other people. He very powerfully demonstrated the power of words. I have a lady friend who is able to channel the singing voice of Maria Callas. When she sings, taking her voice up and down the scale, it has a powerful effect on the listener. She uses her voice as a healing tool for people who are open to such therapy. In this way she uses her voice for the benefit of others. However, we all use the power of spoken words to attract things, or situations, to ourselves, all unknowing of what we are doing, or how."

"How can we possibly do that?" asks Anita

I laugh. "With a bit of persistence. Okay, again I bring you back to the adage; where you focus, energy flows . . . and creates." I chuckle. "I'm sure you will remember this aphorism for the rest of your life. When Carolyn was in her twenties, she was *discovered* and became a photographic model in the Chicago and Cleveland world of advertising. She lived in Shaker Heights, Ohio. She would often take her two whippet sisters on walks that would take her past a long row of beautiful old mansions, with huge gardens. A couple of these mansions she greatly admired, constantly wishing she could go inside and see their interiors. One day her agency called her to do a photo shoot in one of the mansions she had wanted to go into! She created this with focus and desire. A number of years after she quit the advertising industry, she decided to learn to play the piano. The teacher she chose asked Carolyn to visit her for an interview . . . and so she got to enter the other mansion!"

I nod at them. "Actually, you are all doing similar things on a regular basis, without recognising that you are creating the situations. However, we can also create a serious downside with the focus of our repetitive words. One time when I was in Canada, I was speaking on *Focus and the Power of Words*. I was driven to the venue by the wife of a young man who was rather reluctant to be in the audience. 'I'm not into this New Age crap,' he told me, apologetically. After my talk, he came over to me. 'To be honest, I really enjoyed your talk. It set me thinking, and reminded me of a couple of things that have happened in our family,' he said. 'Would you like to hear about it, because I think this is what you may have been talking about?'

I nodded. 'Sure, go ahead.'

He told me how his father was a particularly stubborn man, along with his father's two brothers, his uncles. Really argumentative and difficult men, he told me, all hunters and woodsmen, and convinced that only they were right in just about every situation. His father would be in an argument with somebody on an almost daily basis and he would end it by consistently saying, 'Oh . . . you're just a pain in the neck.' He told me that his father eventually died with cancer of the throat. He then went on to describe his father's older brother, his uncle, who was particularly obdurate. He would end every argument with the words, 'Oh shut up! You're just a pain in the arse.' He died from cancer of the anus. Two slow and very painful deaths, and both men were only in their fifties. The young man then asked me; 'Did they each create the cancers?' I told him a bit more about the power of words and focus. They used words powerfully, brutally and carelessly, and *neck* and *arse* were the focus. I suggested that he draw his own conclusions and to be sure that he did not follow in their footsteps!

"Sadly, people are blinded by their doubts and scepticism. Okay, enough said on this subject," I conclude.

... TEN ...

Work and Working

Then a ploughman said, 'Speak to us of work.'
And he answered saying: *Work is love made visible.*
And if you cannot work with love but only with distaste,
it is better that you should leave your work and sit in the
gate of the temple and take alms of those who work with
joy. For if you bake bread with indifference, you bake a
bitter loaf that feeds but half man's hunger.
And if you grudge the crushing of the grapes, your grudge
distils a poison in the wine.

—Kahlil Gibran

"As LONG WE ARE NOT CONTINUING into any subject matter, this is your opportunity to choose a topic that you wanted to discuss," I suggest.

They all look at me thoughtfully, then glance toward Todd.

Todd takes a deep breath, holds it, then breathes out slowly.

"Okay, it seems that I am the elected spokesman. As we mentioned at the beginning of all this, we are all part of various trained teams within a large organisation that works with disadvantaged people. Some are far less disadvantaged than others, but most of them face challenges of some sort or other. I should add that these are not necessarily mental or emotional disadvantages, but they mostly come from broken homes and parents who were not as caring as they could have been. Sure, this creates emotional problems, but many of these people are very bright." He sighs. "It sometimes seems that the brighter they are, the deeper the hurt.

"Anyway, one of the topics we would like some insight into is the question of work. Some of these people want to work, others don't. Some feel guilty because they don't have jobs, others have parents who never worked, and ask themselves why should *they* work? We do the best we can with all this, but despite our training, sometimes all our logic and explanations seem to be totally inadequate."

"Hmm. I'm impressed. That was very clearly presented," I respond.

"Well . . . to be honest, I work because I need the money," Anita states, "but don't we all? I mean, isn't this something that society has forced onto us? The Aboriginals who used to live here didn't work for a living. They hunted and gathered, and I bet they had far more time to themselves than we do in our clever modern age."

I laugh. "I have no doubt about that. But would you want to live in the conditions in which they lived?"

"No, not in the way that I have been brought up, but if I had been born as one of them, their way of life would be normal and acceptable."

I nod. "Yes, I agree, it would. But you are living now in a so-called civilised world, and it is as it is."

"Why do you call it a *so-called* civilised world?" Anita questions.

I sigh. "We are in danger of going off the topic here, but just briefly, how is a world of rampant poverty, global malnutrition and escalating suicide indicative of a civilised world? How can 'might is right' be civilised? How can a world where ninety-nine percent of the people are controlled by a depraved one percent be called civilised? When pharmaceutical companies have a vested interest in global sickness, ruthlessly suppressing all natural herbal cures, where does civilisation come into the equation? What is civilised about war and warfare and government and corporate corruption? Is that enough?"

Anita nods. "More than enough, I'd say. But just one thing, surely the Western World is not part of the global malnutrition."

"Anita, every person in the Western World who is obese is seriously malnourished. Add to that much of our everyday population is malnourished to one degree or another, in one way or another. Oh yes, we all eat plenty of food, but we seldom concern ourselves about the nutritional content of what we eat. Ask any nutritionist and you may get a surprise. I'm not talking about well fed, I'm taking about full nutrition. Okay?"

Anita is smiling. "Okay . . . I think!"

"Seriously, Anita, we would be a far healthier people if we ate less food but with more complete nutrition."

"Okay, okay . . . I surrender," Anita laughs. "I'm sure you're right."

"Of course I am! So, this takes us back to the question of work. I rather like the words of Kahlil Gibran on work, for they hold the deepest essence of Truth, but I confess, they do not apply to the average person of our times. Very much a Truth out of timing! We live in a society that demands we all work for a living, and in our deeply subconscious way of life, this is not about to change anytime soon. I remember clearly when I worked for a living. I used to milk a herd of about one hundred cows on my dairy farm on the foothills of Mt Arthur, in Tasmania. It was not a labour of love. Even though I really loved my cows, I hated the regimentation of milking, every morning and evening . . . endless and forever, or so it seemed. Anyway, there came a time when I realised that it was fear that cracked the whip; I bent my back to the whiplash of fear and milked the cows. That insight, that unwanted revelation, was a turning point for me. I realised that I did not honour myself, nor the cows, nor my wife and family. Nothing in life was honoured by my action."

"But why should it be?" Todd asks.

"There is no why, Todd. It was just that deep down on a soul level I knew that there was a better way to live. Some few people feel this, others don't. This does not mean that they *should* feel it . . . hmm, it's about timing. I felt it. Eventually, this took me away from farming, vaguely searching for another way of life, of living, even of *being*. I had no clarity on what I was doing, or even on what I was searching for, but that did not stop me . . . and my family had to be a part of this. In hindsight, it was not so good for them, but it was as it was. With a group of like-minded people, my late wife and I started an intentional community, yet four years later we left it, simply because the people of the community and I had a different vision for life. I needed to go. I knew that only I could live my dream, not other people.

"Over a period of a decade or so, all this gradually and eventually led to a breakdown in my health, and at a particular crisis point, I emerged into a completely different, greater reality. Some time later I reluctantly became a so-called spiritual teacher, travelling the world for about fifteen years with my late wife. That time ended with her transition. When, eighteen months later, I was shocked and delighted to once again be in Love, I married the lovely Carolyn. It was then that I embraced and fully committed myself willingly to being that so-called spiritual teacher. It's probably just as well. This year we travelled to five continents and twelve countries. And I am a person who never even wanted to travel! But with Carolyn, it is all wonderful.

"However, my point is this. I no longer work for a living; I now live that I may work. For me, work *truly is* Love made visible. I Love what I do. For me, it is no longer work, even though I put in many hours. It is my life, my passion, my inner growth."

Todd smiles at me knowingly. "I have read some of your books. I read, *A Glimpse of Something Greater*, so I know how much you're not telling us."

"Hmm . . . so it was probably you who suggested that you should all meet with me, huh?"

Todd laughs. "Guilty, as charged. That's why I'm the spokesman."

"So you have briefly outlined to us not so much how you changed your work, but more how *you* changed, and that changed your relationship with work. Would that be a fair summary?" Anita asks.

I nod. "Very astute. I suggest that you attempt to convince people in your workshops, or whatever you do, that their work is fundamentally their meeting place with *life*. When you meet life joyfully through your work, you are going to feel, and be, fulfilled. A person who is fulfilled on a daily basis is a person who is going to grow in consciousness. Consider it this way; we are all in a working partnership with life, and through your work you are honouring yourself *and* life. I have an aphorism about this: *If you honour self, you honour life. If you honour life, life will honour you.* The workplace is a very potent arena in which to create this alchemy."

"Apart from you, does anybody look at work like this?" Anita asks.

I nod. "You might be surprised. I have spoken to a few real estate agents who really love what they do. I remember listening to one such woman telling me what a kick she got out of matching a person or family with a house. She did not focus on selling the house, but more on matching people with the perfect house for *them*. The result, a very high success rate in selling houses. Most real estate agents try to sell houses, but not her. She scarcely gave it a thought. She turned her work into her pleasure and passion, while another turns it into a burden and a drudge. It is not about the work, it is about the *attitude* to work."

"I like what you are saying," Todd says, nodding. "It makes so much sense, but I do wonder how easy or difficult it would be, or will be, to instil such ideas in jobless people. Especially the long-term unemployed."

"If it were me – and it is not – I would pick out the people who you consider are open and receptive to such ideas and work with them to an extra degree. When you get a breakthrough success with a few of them, you will have role models for the other people. You then get them to tell their stories of how they not only broke the stalemate of long-term unemployment, but also found work that they actually enjoy.

"Nothing succeeds like success . . . even if it is an illusion."

"What do you mean by that?" Anita instantly asks.

I wave it away. "Nothing, a throw away remark. Forget it."

"I don't believe that for a second, so you might as well explain it." Anita replies, firmly. "Come on . . . give!"

She is persistent. "Okay, but enough of just standing around. Let's go and sit on the edge of the big pond. Then we'll go indoors again."

I call it the big pond, even though it is smaller than the converted pool/pond. It took me weeks to build the multi-sized chunks of granite stone into a retaining wall, so it *felt* bigger! It is built on soft rock, so instead of going *down* into the soil, I had to build it *up* from the rock. With its paved capping on the granite, it makes for comfortable seating.

When everyone was settled, I mentally reprimanded my loose tongue, while considering the quickest possible explanation for my remark.

"Right . . . nothing in Nature has any reference for success or failure. They are both human concepts based on single physical lives and on judging those lives. Make a huge amount of money and be an extremely unpleasant, disliked person, yet you are a success. Make just enough money to humbly live on your income and be revered and loved by all who know you, and you are a failure. How stupid is this? This is human folly, judging failure and success. When you have lived ten thousand lifetimes, ranging across almost every experience available to a creative human . . . what does success and failure mean? It means nothing, other than the judgement of those who are critical, foolish and ignorant."

"I like what you are saying," Todd says again, "but what do you do in the situation where a person hates their work? I don't mean hates working, but simply hates the work they are doing?"

"Hmm . . . yes, an all too common scenario. There is no single answer to this, because it depends so much on the openness and flexibility of the person or people involved. If the person who is in a job they hate is open, I would recommend that they attempt to change their attitude to their work. For some, this makes a huge difference and the work may become acceptable, but for others it makes no difference at all. If they continue to detest their work, it is important to quit. This takes courage, because of the threat of becoming, and maybe remaining, unemployed. This is the tricky part. If you believe that it will be difficult to get another job, it will be. If you believe that you will easily get another job, you will. What you believe and emotionally focus on determines the outcome of what you will create in your life.

"On the other hand, if you stay in a job you hate because of the fear of not having an income, then this becomes a form of subconscious self-attack. It equates to five days working and hating it, then the weekend off, and back to the self-punishment. This creates a repetitive and unpleasant life; one that is all too common. These people easily get sick, constantly taking paid leave!"

Todd nods. "Yeah, I get it. A multiplicity of people means that no single technique is going to fix it. And fear and insecurity play a big role in this."

"They certainly do," I reply. "A *very* big role. However, I will add that oftentimes people will have a job that they do not particularly enjoy, but is not something that they hate. Usually they have responsibilities to the home and family, and this is often their life lesson; to stay with a work situation to care for their family and see to their welfare, before catering to their own wants and desires. The difficulty is in sorting out which of these categories, and the many other groups, the people you are helping belong in. I don't envy you this task."

I smile all round. "Okay, people, time for another topic."

... ELEVEN ...

Fear and Insecurity

Fear lives in the shadows of your life, snarling and threatening you into a state of terror. Once you create the courage within yourself to shine a light into the shadows, it is fear that will skulk away, tail tucked between its legs. The only power fear has over you is the power you give it.

—Michael J. Roads

THE GROUP ALL LOOK at Todd once more.

He smiles. "Well . . . I just said it, didn't I? Fear and insecurity. These are very real human problems in all of us, not just those people who are struggling with work issues."

He looks at me, mildly embarrassed. "I definitely have this problem."

"I'm sure you do. Like you said, along with most of humanity. Let me say at the very beginning of this – at the risk I might repeat myself, which will be all to the good – *fear is not real*. Fear has no place in reality at all. Fear is always based in illusion."

I pause, waiting for the protests.

Peter obliges, jumping to his feet to vigorously object. "I find that very

59

difficult to believe or accept. Everyone has fear of some type or another. Fear is a natural part of our lives, and is very real."

I seem to spend a lot of time sighing! Why is it so difficult for people who want to learn, to listen? Why do dysfunctional people who know nothing of life think that they are right? It does not make sense. But then, of course, neither do irrational and dysfunctional people!

"Back to choices. Either you listen to me, or you depart. I have better things to do with my day than listen to babes telling Grandpa how life works!"

Todd looks angry. "Sit down, Peter . . . and shut up! If you want to take one of the cars, take mine and go. I fully intend to stay."

White-faced with anger and red with embarrassment, creating an odd splotchy effect on the skin of his face, Peter sits a fair distance away, but well within the range of my voice.

I look at Todd. "Don't be too hard on Peter. Fear is frequently generated and greatly misunderstood by most people. It certainly seems natural enough, and fear is so constantly in attendance that many people even call it *my* fear. This is not a good idea; people are attached enough to fear as it is, without needing to *own* it. Someone once coined the phrase; F E A R – False Evidence Appearing Real. This is brilliant, and accurate. Fear always appears as though it is real, yet it only has the reality that we create for it.

"We are creators; we create fear. God did not create fear and give us all a large dollop of it! Yet, as is obvious, there have to be reasons for this very negative mis-creation that messes up so many lives, binding us into servitude to illusion. So let's look a bit more deeply into this. This is what I have learned from my metaphysical investigation into the fear phenomenon. Physiologists may not agree with me, nor medical science, so please feel free to disregard my words. It is very well documented that we all have a divided brain; the left hemisphere and the right hemisphere. They are connected by the corpus callosum and are designed to work as one cohesive whole. Unfortunately, the deliberate and conscious use of our whole-brain is rather uncommon. Throughout the last two hundred thousand year cycle of humanity – and other human cycles have preceded this – we have become increasingly left-brain dominant. By this I don't mean that we are *unable* to be whole-brain, or that we do not use the right-brain, I simply mean left-brain dominant."

I pause. "Maybe you are familiar with this?"

Glancing at the group, Marsha speaks up. "We are not unfamiliar with the brain hemispheres and left-brain dominance, but I figure this is leading somewhere. I would like to know where!"

I nod. "Good. The left-brain is about survival, competition, aggression, and fighting . . . along with other qualities such as the intellect. Basically, it has all the survival characteristics that we need. There was once a time when survival was of paramount importance, but that time passed long ago. We are immortal Beings, so I ask you, how rational is this fear to survive?"

"Surely you are aware that people do not walk around thinking of their immortality," Peter said, cynically. "They mostly feel vulnerable and afraid."

"More is the pity," I reply. "Personally, I live constantly aware of my immortality and I have no fear. Or, to be very accurate, when a crisis moment comes – and I do get them – I do not choose fear, I choose Love."

"I believe you," says Marsha, "but *how* do you do this? As I listen to you and think about this, I don't see how it is possible."

"Remember what I said earlier; you cannot listen and think, in the way that you just claimed," I say, smiling at her. "I'll continue. My metaphysical investigation indicates that under a certain degree of stress, the left-brain produces an energy that is composed of minute amounts of hormone and bio-chemical secretions, while also composed of metaphysical energy of a very low frequency. This alchemical brew has a startling effect on the body/mind. We name it . . . fear. The truth is that the whole body has a very negative reaction to fear. Every cell becomes more acidic, more rigid, less efficient and more vulnerable to disease."

"And yet fear saves lives," Peter says, obstinately.

I chuckle. "Oh, do you mean running away to fight another day? Or running away from an attacking tiger? You mean things like that?"

"Yes . . . that sort of thing saves lives," he replies, defensively.

"Okay, let's be clear about this. You can lose your body/identity, but you cannot lose your life. *You are life*. It is not possible to lose it. In the illusion, people believe in, and act out, the pantomime of being a mortal body, so they are very fearful of death and dying. The left-brain has a deeply ingrained subconscious program of fight, flight, or freeze . . . survival. The left-brain believes that their persona identity and the body are self. And it acts on this deep subconscious program of belief. I *know* that this is not who I am. I *know* that I am not a mortal physical body, so this deep *knowing* gives me freedom from fear. My *knowing* is far greater than a common belief which is devoid of Truth."

"So your knowledge is like a freedom?" Anita asks.

"No. This is not a long-established knowledge – I have mentioned this – it is my in-the-moment *knowing*. You have to experience the difference to fully appreciate just how great the difference is. It is neither rational nor logical."

Todd eyes me shrewdly. "So by living in the illusion, I maintain and even create my fears, yes?"

I give him my best smile. "Yes, Todd. That's exactly right. If you cross the threshold from illusion to a greater reality, you go from fear to Love. However, be aware that fear is not the opposite of Love. Love has no opposite, although sadly, it does have opposition. Incredibly, we, who are creations of Love, are also the opposition to Love! Clever us, huh!"

"So dealing with our fears also deals with our insecurities?" Anita asks.

I nod. "Top of the class! How can you have fears and not be insecure? Equally, how could you be insecure without fear? It is very well documented that those with great wealth are often insecure. You cannot buy fearlessness! You cannot buy unconditional Love. You cannot buy inner peace. You cannot buy inner freedom. You cannot buy Truth. All these come with the journey of an ascending state of consciousness. Understandably, most people are hooked on an ascending income, rather than on an ascending soul."

Marsha takes a deep breath. "You honestly and truly don't experience or feel fear? I mean, how do you do this? My mind goes blank when I even try to think about it!"

I smile at her sympathetically. "I can see your quandary. To be honest, there was a time when my fear levels were so high and so constant that I also would not have believed anyone telling me what I am now telling you! At an Intensive I often jokingly say that by the time I was forty-nine and three months, my fear quota had been so overused it was completely used up! I know the taste of fear, make no mistake about that. But, as an enlightened man, and a man who experiences unconditional Love, fear no longer has a place in my life. I choose Love. Where there is Love, there is no fear."

"Suppose you were about to be shot?" Anita asks, with a chuckle.

"I can only surmise the situation, but I'm sure that I would feel regret. I dearly Love my beautiful Carolyn and would deeply regret leaving her, but it would only be for a moment of timelessness and we would be together once more. You need to realise that if I died fearfully, then I would incarnate back into another life of opportunities to again choose fear. If I died without fear, feeling only Love for the shooter, I move on into a life of higher vibrations. I repeat, we are the creators of our eternal lives. We create the direction and the content of all our lives in the way that we live in the eternal moment."

"All I can say is . . . like, wow!" Anita replies. "I find even the concept of having no fear utterly amazing, I can't imagine the reality of it."

"I understand." I say. "Long ago, so we are told, the early Christians were given a choice in the public arena. Renounce God in front of the crowds and live, or own your God, and be killed and eaten by the lions. I have no idea of the statistics, but apparently many chose to own God as their saviour, and were torn to pieces and eaten by the lions. A very nasty death. My point is this: without a shadow of doubt, they were terrified by the prospect, fearful beyond measure, but they did it anyway. They didn't deny their fear, but they also didn't let it rule their lives. I am in awe of that level of courage."

"So it's not about not having fear that is important, it is about not allowing fear to control you?" Anita says, triumphantly.

I beam at her. "Yes, Anita. This is what it is about. When you deny fear the right to control your life, you will learn what a toothless tiger it truly is."

Todd looks relieved. "I could do this. In fact, *I will do it*."

"And once you begin to do this, fear will gradually lose its grip on you and your life will change for the better. Fear lives in the shadows of your life, snarling and threatening you into a state of terror. Once you create the courage within yourself to shine a light into the shadows, it is fear that will skulk away, tail tucked between its legs. The only power fear has over you is the power you give it. How do we do this? By creating a powerful, negatively imagined scenario of the situation or person that threatens us . . . in this way we create and maintain fear. We can just as easily reverse this, by powerfully imagining a positive outcome to the situation or person. We are the creator! Do you get it? We – you and I – we are the creators of our life."

"Let me give you my version of F E A R – Face it, Evaluate, Act, Relax. Remembering all I have told you, face the fears and decide what you are going to do about them. Then act upon it, and relax . . . *trustingly*."

... TWELVE ...

Life and Living – Death and Dying

*When you live in such a way that you know what life
actually is, then you will find that you know death in the
same way, even when alive in the body. Death is not
the end. Death is an aspect of the living of life. When
you shed your physical mortal body, you will be more
fully alive than you have experienced in a long time.*
—Michael J. Roads

I SMILE AT THEM, noticing that they are all – even Peter – fully engaged
by my words. It is obvious that his resistance, his fear, is getting a shake-
up.

Standing up, I make the suggestion that we go and sit on the deck. This
is our indoor/outdoor room. The house roof covers it, but two sides are
open, having fly-screening instead of glass. It's a very comfortable summer
room.

They follow me to the deck and we all get comfortably seated. Carolyn
joins us, once again making the offer of coffee or tea, this time accompanied
by cake. Everyone is ready for more refreshments.

"Okay, so what's the next item on your list?" I ask.

With the exception of Peter, they all put their heads together, whispering to each other. It does not take them long to come to a decision.

"We all basically vote to let you take the conversation where you think best," Todd says. "We think we know certain things and you then show us that we really don't. That's both illuminating and challenging. So although it obviously pushes buttons, it seems we learn better this way."

Hmm . . . how am I supposed to know what they need? They like to be challenged . . . that should not be too difficult! Ah, I know a way.

"A good subject to get to the nitty-gritty of life and living is death and dying. Are you open to this?"

"I'm not sure how you get to the essence of life and living through death and dying, it sounds like a complete oxymoron to me. But yes, we are open to anything you choose," Todd replies, cautiously.

"I've suggested this because modern humanity has no idea how to die these days. Most people die in enormous discomfort at the very least, or in serious pain, controlled only by drugs. I acknowledge that a few people quietly die in their sleep, but they are a tiny minority. We have no idea how to die, simply because we have no idea how to live. Living and dying hold hands. If you live in a way that does not work, you will almost certainly die in a similar manner. This maintains our fear. You see? I cannot separate one subject from another. Fear leads to dying badly, hence I decided to follow the connection from our previous conversation."

"My father died terribly from cancer," Peter says, quietly.

I nod sympathetically. "So did mine. About fifty-five years ago from cancer of the pancreas, and it still kills most people who get it. I know we all like to blame sickness on an outside agency, like *catching* it, but we don't catch cancer, we create it through living in a way that does not work. If you remember, I told you that we have two ways of living. About ninety-four percent of people live in a way that does not work for their overall well-being, so they get sick . . . and die."

"Where do you get that ninety-four percent figure from?" Peter asks.

I smile at him. "Top psychologists generally agree that an estimated ninety-four percent of humanity live subconsciously for about ninety percent of their lives. This does not work; they are the sick majority. We are born and designed to live consciously. All Nature lives consciously. Why would anyone think that living less than fully consciously is better? The question to ask is *why* does humanity live this way?"

"Okay, I'll buy it," Anita smiles. "I'm asking why?"

"You see, if you were listening earlier, you would know why, because I've already answered this question. Nevertheless, I'll answer it again. We think and we seldom stop thinking. You can think your way out of the moment, but you cannot think your way into it. Remember?"

Peter and Todd nod, while the others shake their heads.

"Inadvertently, living subconsciously creates stress in people's lives, stress they are mostly unaware of. If you were able to see the stress with metaphysical vision, it looks rather like a shadow-self, and it is negative. Not negative because all such people are negative, but negative as in being polarised, like a magnet. In a like manner, being conscious creates a positive effect. The *long-term* stress from our subconscious conditioning has a detrimental effect, shortening lives and causing illness. Of course, I am at risk of people not believing this, but unfortunately not believing something does not change the reality. And this is a reality that only a few people are aware of. The day will come when it is not X-rays and MRI scans and suchlike that will determine our condition, but metaphysical energy scans."

"So . . . being subconscious does not mean that we are compelled to be a negative person?" Anita asks. "I need that clarified."

"Not at all. You can be a lifelong positive person and live a productive life, but your metaphysical energy will be affected by the polarisation effect."

"So when you said you never get tired, is this one of the reasons why? You live more consciously and reap the benefits," Anita exclaims.

"Yes, this is true. I am free of the energetic stress that accompanied me for many years. That energetic stress actually is an energy drain. Yet, like it or not, we have created it. It is a fact that, cell for cell, most animals have far more energy than humans do. But potentially, our energy can be by far the greatest, as it certainly should be."

"Are you conscious all the time?" Peter asks.

"No, I am not. Like every aware person on this planet, I am growing in consciousness, and this is very important to me. I am more conscious than most people and I am conscious for most of the time, but I have a way to go."

"Who would be more conscious than you?" Anita asks.

"All the great Masters through the ages, like Jesus, Buddha, and others of that ilk. And there are people alive today who are not public figures – quite the opposite, in fact – who are more fully conscious than I am."

"Who are they? I've never heard of them," Anita asks.

"That's because they are hidden away in very remote places."

"Why are they hidden away?" Anita chimes in.

"Simply because they consciously merge their elevated consciousness into the overall consciousness of humanity with the pure intent of elevating it. We need such people, comparative few as they are. Hidden away from the mainstream of humanity they can do this undisturbed. We need them."

"Okay, I'll be dumb," Anita chuckles, "so why are you a public figure if you enjoy your privacy like you mentioned?"

I laugh. "I oftentimes ask myself the same question. This is my choice. I have a gift of communication, verbal and written. So I use it. I enjoy what I do, but I do appreciate my privacy. However, I blend public and private easily.

"Now, let's get back to our topic. Animals live approximately seven times longer than the time it takes to fully develop their physical body. This can vary in different animals, but it is a fair, overall basic measure. We humans are mostly fully developed in about twenty years. Okay, we may put weight on, or lose it, but you get the idea. This indicates that if we were to live seven times twenty, we would live around one hundred and forty years! But we do not. Why not? Because we live *out* of the moment, hence less energy, greater stress, shorter lives. By contrast, within Nature, all animals live *in* the eternal moment, the place of full energy."

All five are staring at me in bewilderment. "That is amazing!" Marsha declares. "Utterly, scarily, amazing."

"If it's true," Peter adds, cynically.

"As I said, taking the approximate overall life spans of most of the various species of mammals, you will find it to be fairly accurate. Living in the moment consciously is a very different experience of life than from living out of the moment subconsciously. Do you honestly believe that God created animals to live a full life, and us to live a half-life? Or do you suppose that we might possibly be the masters of self-sabotage?"

Marsha stares at me. "You're a scary person to talk to. Before we came here I was living happily in my little bubble of delusion. Now you've burst it. So now what do I do?"

I smile at her. "You can resurrect it, and crawl back into its confinement and limits, or you can stay out, take a deep breath, and begin a new life."

She laughs. "I'll take the new life."

"Will you? Are you sure? Because the new life has to be lived as a new person. A Truth is not a Truth unless you are *living* it. A week from now, when you have had time to resurrect old thoughts and habits, and it's so easy to creep back into sameness, you might remember my words. It takes courage and effort to create and maintain positive change in your life."

"What would it take to live like you?" Todd asks.

"You need to remember that in this life I began this path about fifty years ago. And I have had many incarnations as a wandering mystic, mostly coming to a very nasty physical end. But that did not take away the soul growth I experienced. I was a seeker for a very long time. I no longer *seek*. I simply *grow* from my conscious relationship with the moment of life. You can do the same, despite your personal history. If you were truly interested, I would suggest you attend an Intensive. You will learn a way of life and living that, should you care enough to live it, will set you free. But, and it's a big but, you are required to *live* what you learn. Spiritual knowledge holds and offers no freedom, only the living actualisation of it will do this.

"When you live in such a way that you *know* what life actually is, then you will find that you *know* death in the same way, even when alive in the body. Death is not the end. Death is an aspect of the living of life. When you shed your physical, mortal body, you will be more fully alive than you have experienced for a long time. However, I have to say that dying and death are no more the same for all people than is life and living. A person who has achieved self-Love will experience a very different death process than those people who dislike themselves. And they will have different experiences when they leave the physical body. We are the creators of the *entirety* of our lives, not just the physical part of it.

"I often smile when I hear people describe a transcendent moment, calling it a near-*death* experience. In truth, what they experienced was a near-*life* experience; the rest of their life was a near-death experience! It never ceases to amaze me how most people live their mortal and physical lives blind to the beauty and illumination of a greater metaphysical reality. It is rather like living a black and white monochrome photograph compared with one lived in full, glorious colour. Even our greatest, most transcendent experiences do not compare with the clarity and sheer magnificence of a greater reality, to all of which most of humanity are blind and unaware."

"What do we have to do to . . . er, connect with this greater reality? Is there any technique, or method to put us in touch with it?" Todd asks.

"It's not a matter of techniques; it's a matter of living Truth. If you were to meet a caterpillar and have a chat with it, you would find that it has no concept of its butterfly potential. Colourful, a caterpillar may be, but nothing in its 'crawling' life can compare with the flight of the butterfly. However, because of a biological program, the caterpillar will eventually metamorphose into the butterfly, so it *will* experience its full potential. We do not have a biological program that will transform us into our Light-Selves. We will remain stuck as the caterpillar-self until such time that we consciously choose to develop our potential and ascend into our Light-Self. And being conscious is the key. While people live subconsciously, so we live within the confines of the illusion. This is the home of the caterpillar-self. When people choose to live more consciously, and practice being conscious, so we open the inner eyes to a greater reality and our Light-Self."

"So the technique is . . . er, being conscious?" Anita says.

I sigh. "No, my dear. Being conscious is not a technique. Being fully conscious is the only way of living that works. Techniques have a use-by date, while living consciously increases your ability to consciously live. In this way you grow in consciousness until you reach the stage where illusions fall away and life stands revealed in a greater reality."

"But, er . . . what is a greater reality?" Anita asks, desperately. "I'm trying to understand, I really am, but I just don't get it."

I smile at her. "Anita, you are never going to understand. And even if you thought you did, what you thought would eventually be revealed as false. When you experience a greater reality you will realise just how futile attempting to understand it actually is. Understanding is all about the mind attempting to put a hook into something that it cannot experience. The mind can be an onlooker, but not a participant. It can make statements about what is happening to the soul, but it is not the soul having the experience."

Grinning at me, Anita gives a hugely exaggerated sigh. "So are you telling me that you do not understand the daily events in your life?"

"Oh God, give me patience! No . . . I am not telling you that. Of course I understand the events in my life. Our *intellectual* life naturally embraces understanding, okay! No problems there. Our *spiritual* life moves on a very different wave of energy. It is based in intelligence, not the intellect. Intellect is the domain of understanding. Yes? Intelligence is the domain of experiencing.

They occupy different energy waves in our life. For too many people, the wave of the intellect is very dominant, while for too few people, intelligence is their wave of reality."

...THIRTEEN...

On Marriage

And a person said, 'Master, speak to us of marriage.'
And he answered saying: *You were born together,*
and together you shall be forever more.
You shall be together when the white wings of death
scatter your days. Aye, you shall be together even in
the silent memory of God.
But let there be spaces in your togetherness, and let
the winds of heaven dance between you.

—Kahlil Gibran

"OKAY, LET'S MOVE THIS ALONG. Next topic, please."

Marsha gives me a shrewd look. "You're an older man. I would like to hear your views on marriage. As you are aware, many people don't bother with marriage these days. What do think about this?"

I chuckle. "To answer your second question first, I really don't think about it at all. How people chose to live is of very little concern to me. But my views on marriage, now that's a reasonable question.

"I am a married man by choice. When I married my late wife, I was twenty-one. Marriage was something that you did. Living together was very frowned upon in those days, so most couples got married. To be honest, the marriage ceremony itself meant little to me, except that I could now have unlimited legitimate sex! Nevertheless, I liked the idea of being married and that my wife and I were now recognised as a married couple. As it turned out, I proved to be very good at marriage. I quickly learned that a happy wife was a happy home. I don't mean a spoiled-rotten wife, but a respected, happy and loving wife treated me in a way that I enjoyed. And then there is the aspect of Love. I loved my wife from the moment I first met her. Over the years I learned that my early love was very much a puppy love, but as I matured it developed into as real a Love as I could manage. When she died after forty-nine years of marriage, I was devastated."

"How did you deal with that," Marsha asks, sympathetically.

"As a spiritual teacher and an enlightened man, I had many more inner resources to draw upon than the average person. I did not believe in death, any more than did my late wife. She began to communicate with me within three days of departing. She was so very happy, even though sad for me. But all that is another documented story. (*Through the Eyes of Love; Journeying with Pan; Book One*). Because I live the spiritual Truths that I teach and *know*, I was aware of the bigger picture in a greater reality. Add to this the fact that I focused on learning and growing through the experience of my deep loss. These factors made a huge difference, so within a year I was through the major part of my grieving.

"Carolyn was my Intensive organiser in America and had just gone through a separation with her husband. When we came together for my Intensive the following year – I travelled alone for the first time – a fifteen-year friendship/love suddenly and very surprisingly blossomed into a deep and romantic Love. Within a few months we were married. However my second marriage was very different."

"How so?" Anita pops in.

"Well . . . as Carolyn put it, we were two mature adults, we did not *need* to get married. So she was very surprised when I proposed marriage to her. Of course, she accepted, and then I told her why. Marriage to me was a small public witnessing of our joining of energies. Marriage creates a sacred energetic connection and I greatly honour this. Within the marriage vows it is normal that a commitment is made between the couple. If at any stage of the relationship between a married couple there are problems or personal conflict, a true commitment between two people creates an energetic bridge across the space between them, so that they can use this sacred space to once again reconnect. Let me be clear that a commitment is not just a matter of saying some words to each other. Carolyn and I wrote the words of our marriage vows, and when we spoke them before an assembled group of family and friends – witnesses – we were both conscious and sincere, fully comprehending the meaning and implications of the words that we spoke to each other."

"So you could say that your first wedding was a subconscious one, while your second was more conscious," Marsha declares.

I look at her in surprise. "Hmm . . . very good! I had never even thought of it that way, or considered it like that, but yes, you stated it brilliantly.

"We are living in times when many couples separate because the marriage gets rather difficult. Then, months or years later, they often get involved with someone else, simply living together. This is not a good idea. When you are married in a witnessed ceremony, the energies of the marrying couple come together . . . and they stay together. Later, despite the physical bodies going through a separation, on a metaphysical level their energies remain connected. I have had friends in this predicament. I generally suggest that they go through a proper divorce, which is a brief formal process that erases the energetic, metaphysical connection. When they do this they are always amazed at the feeling of freedom they feel. People do not *see* this energetic connection, but when we make it, we are required to unmake it!"

"That's amazing," Anita exclaims.

"Let me tell you a little marriage story. When my youngest son got married for the first time, he asked me to be his best man. I was honoured. After the wedding I had a few words with him: 'Russ, you are now wedded. In somewhere around two- to three-years' time, your *real* marriage will begin. This is a wedding ceremony we have just had, and wonderful as it was, a wedding does not a marriage make!'

"He was unimpressed with my wisdom. 'Oh, Dad, whatever are you talking about? I'm a married man . . . now.'

"I smiled and shrugged. 'You'll see.'

"One day, nearly two and a half years later, Russ said to me: 'Dad, do you remember at my wedding what you said to me about how my marriage would be another couple of years or so before it kicked in? What made you say that?'

"'Simple enough,' I replied. 'The first two years are all about sex. Sex is so delightful that it fills in most of your spare moments, and most arguments are quickly dissolved in the frenzy of sex. However, after a couple of years, sex is no longer quite enough, unless you are both fully compatible. After a couple of years, you realise that you are really and truly married and that there needs to be more between you than *just* sex. You've tried every possible sexual position, and every place in the house, but now you need something more. I know, Russ, I've been there! So . . . you have a problem?'

He grinned at me. 'Yeah . . . we've reached the place where we are having to work at our marriage. You were right. I'm now in the *real* marriage.'"

I smile at Anita. "Are you married?"

"No. I have a partner and we live together." She grimaced at me. "Oh God . . . what are you going to tell me now?"

I laughed. "Nothing; your life is your business, not mine. But I will say this much; many partnership couples have a far deeper and more meaningful relationship than do the marriages of some people. A marriage is not about the wedding, it is about the measure of Love between the couple. If Love is in a marriage, so be it, and if Love is in a partnership, so be it. Many people will seek marriage just to feel more emotionally secure. This does not make for a good marriage. And quite often the person they attract will have the same problem. Two emotionally insecure people together is no easier than being insecure alone! In these modern times many people want a relationship, and quite often, even basic human love is not involved. Not the best idea.

"If you wait a moment, I will read out to you the words that I wrote a few years ago for the marriage of my niece. I'll go and get it."

"Okay," I say upon my return, "you may empathise with it, you may not, but it is advice toward creating and maintaining a long-term marriage, or relationship. And you can consider this my last words on the topic. I call it marriage wisdom."

MARRIAGE WISDOM

A MARRIAGE BETWEEN A COUPLE is rather like the marriage of an eagle to the rising thermals of warm air. As the eagle takes its first leap from the branch of a tree, its wings clutch the air with a mighty effort: once, twice, even three times this may happen, then the miracle of flight takes over as the eagle rises on the warm currents. So too, it is with marriage. If you use the skills that are inherent in all of us, you will both need to make the occasional mighty effort not to get angry, not to get impatient, and to really understand this person to whom you are now married. Then, with effortless effort, you catch the uplifting thermals of honour and respect, and together, lift yourselves and your marriage to a new and higher expression of Love. You can only do this by being truly aware of this other, very different person in your life, and being aware of their own, unique needs.

There are three basic skills you each need for your marriage to fly to its full and potential height: Commitment, Communication, and Consideration. When you are truly committed to your marriage partner, you invoke a higher order of expression. Although this higher order may not carry you through the rough squalls of marriage, it *will* enable you to find a greater capacity within yourselves, enabling you to deal with any relevant issues. Together, you will fly through the storms that you each encounter as you lift your marriage even higher. Put simply, this is the process of spiritual growth. You must also realise that your partner really cannot read your mind, and that you need to learn the skill of *communicating* your Love, along with the much more difficult skill of communicating the fears that arise from your everyday life. Yes, we all have our fears, and sharing them with your partner-in-love helps to empty these fears of any power they may hold over you. Then there is consideration . . . for all the times when you need to consider your beloved partner's needs before your own, when your care and concern for your partner is the absolving and forgiving hug, or the strong and loving shoulder on which they can safely lean.

Commitment to your beloved partner, communication of both the joys and sorrows of life, and a deep consideration for each other. All these are needed as you clutch the potential of your togetherness, making the effort needed to rise even higher on the thermals of Love, into a fine and glorious marriage. Like the eagle riding the height of the sky-waves, so too, a marriage can be the effortless soaring of two people on the rare thermals of unconditional Love. And it is Love without conditions which will ultimately define your marriage.

This is the potential of your marriage. May you both fly high.

(I give full permission for anyone to use this at their own wedding.)

...FOURTEEN...

On Relationships

Your relationship with yourself is your relationship with life. This relationship will define your abundance – and I do not mean wealth – or your poverty, your good or bad health, and all your relationships with other people. From experience, I can tell you that most people have an angry, critical and judgemental relationship with themselves, full of fear, blame, guilt and remorse. Definitely not all people, but far too many. This does not work!

—Michael J. Roads

"Wow . . . I really like that," Anita exclaims. "It's so poetic."

"Not surprisingly. I have written a fair bit of poetry and, more recently, I am writing lyrics. Okay, so after marriage comes . . . what?"

"How about relationships?" Marsha asks. "I know there is a similarity to marriage, but relationships include all of us, and go every which way."

"Hmm . . . you're correct, of course. Almost everyone is in some sort of relationship with someone, and most of us with quite a number of people, like family, friends, work-colleagues and so forth."

"As far as I am concerned, most people have many rather troubled relationships," Marsha continues. "I help people deal with some of them. It is not uncommon for grown-up children to be estranged from a parent, or reject a parent, or be rejected. Then there are the people who seem to hate just about everyone, and are angry and aggressive. Yet, in one way or another, these people are in various relationships, or are trying to be!"

"I have seen how volatile such relationships can be." I sigh. "I'm aware that you are all taught modern ways and means of helping people to deal with their relationship issues, and I have no intention of intruding on these. But how you deal with it depends very much on the hoped for, or needed, outcome of the people within the relationship. I . . ."

"I'm not sure what you mean by that," Anita interjects.

I nod. "Fair enough. Most parents love their children. Okay, this is not a given, but it is normal, even if the way they relate to their children carries a different message. For example, my father never told me that he loved me. I was hurt by this. However, as a grown man, and with the experience I have gleaned in running my Intensives, I am certain he did not say such words simply because he was a male who could not speak of love to another male, no matter the age or relationship. Stupid, yes, but very real, especially in that generation. As a result, he and I were not close and this did not help."

I smile whimsically. "Because he was unable to speak of Love to me, I made very sure to speak words of Love to my four children as they grew up. I still do given the opportunity."

I chuckle. "As the son, I felt rejected by my father. In recent years, as a father, I have been rejected by a son. So I have experienced it both ways."

"Why have you been rejected? I'm amazed that such a thing could happen to you?" Marsha says.

I smile at her. "You know, if, at an Intensive, I want to push a man's buttons, all I need do is ask him about his relationship with his son, or his father. I rarely do this, but on that rare occasion, he will often be close to tears. Sometimes, of course, the relationship is good, but all too often it is not. My son has been angry with me since he was about fifteen years old. It seems that anything and everything that is wrong in his life is my fault, while all the good things in his life are all credit to him!

"But that's so unfair and ridiculous. Doesn't this cause you enormous emotional pain and suffering?" Anita asks, looking concerned.

"It did," I answer, truthfully. "He offered me pain and hurt in an explosive row between us and I took it. After about six months of inner hurt, I realised that it did not have to be this way. Instead, I took a giant step and chose to Love him *unconditionally.* Now, how he chooses to treat me has nothing to do with me, it's *his* choice, *his* stuff. I seriously doubt that I will ever see him again – it has been years – and I'm okay with it. Is this my preference? No, but unconditional Love means no conditions. My life is more peaceful without such an explosive and aggressive relationship in it, so I'm okay with it. I Love him, and I shall continue to Love him for the beautiful soul that I know he is. The angry, aggressive, unpleasant personality is a stranger to me. He is in a new marriage to a lovely woman – so I am told – and I wish him a wonderful life. I can only hope that it transforms him. To me, my son is a loved soul and on a soul level we are very much at peace."

"Wow . . . how do you get to such a place?" Marsha asks.

"By constantly and consciously choosing Love," I reply. "Everyone is in a relationship with themselves. No one can avoid it. This is how I got to such a place that I can experience unconditional Love. I Love myself, fully and unconditionally. I can say the worst possible thing at the worst possible moment, and know that I have seriously put my foot in it . . . and it is as it is. This happens. I do not criticise myself, berate myself, judge myself, none of those. I simply say, 'Okay Michael, you goofed . . . now do your best to put it right.' And I do!"

"Nobody gives much thought to the relationship with themselves," Anita says, thoughtfully. "Or at least, I haven't."

"Actually, more and more people *are* resonating with a great truth," I tell her. "Your relationship with yourself is your relationship with life. This relationship will define your abundance – and I do not mean wealth – or your poverty, your good or bad health, and all your relationships with other people. This indicates, of course, that my son's problem is not in his relationship with me, but in his relationship with himself. And this is so very common in daily life. From experience, I can tell you that most people have an angry, critical and judgemental relationship with themselves, full of fear, blame, guilt and remorse. Definitely not all people, but far, far too many. This does not work!

"This negative relationship with self strongly links to the present day sickness in humanity. How can you thrive when you subconsciously despise yourself? You can't, but as you probably know, this is a common scenario in people. Self-hate and self-attack are the seeds of sickness."

"This is what we work with," Todd says. "A person who is self-loving is a person who is rarely in trouble. With others, we see the self-hate hidden beneath the surface. One wrong word and we see it all come spilling out."

I nod. "Having a relationship with yourself that fulfils you in daily life, while also honouring you in each moment, means that practically all stress disappears out of your life. And really, this is not so very difficult. Most people live a *reactive* life, negatively reacting to the comments and situations of daily life. It is better by far to live in a more *responsive* way. Fear reacts, while love responds. This works!

"Okay, next topic folks."

... FIFTEEN ...

Crime and Punishment

One of the judges asked, 'Master, speak to us of crime and punishment.' And he answered saying: *Oftentimes have I heard you speak of one who commits a wrong as though he were not one of you, but a stranger unto you and an intruder upon your world.*
But I say that even as the holy and the righteous cannot rise beyond the highest which is in each of you, so the wicked and the weak cannot fall lower than the lowest which is in you also. And as a single leaf turns not yellow but with the silent knowledge of the whole tree, so the wrong-doer cannot do wrong without the hidden will of you all.

—Kahlil Gibran

TODD SPEAKS UP ONCE MORE. "Our type of work sometimes gets us involved in the crimes that a few of our people have committed, or even may commit while involved with us. What is your view of our modern system of crime and punishment?"

I stare at him in surprise. "Hmm . . . I must admit that I did not expect crime and punishment to be a subject. But, I have to say that it is one that

I have often reflected on. On a more physical level, I greatly approve of the idea and implementation of community work as a punishment for crimes against the people. Especially minor crimes, which, I suspect, are the majority. I also think it is the perfect punishment for all non-violent crimes.

"However, you are not asking for my *opinion* on our system of crime and punishment, you are asking for my metaphysical viewpoint. Interestingly, I have been formally requested to do jury duty three times. Each time I have agreed to do this, so long as they understand my terms."

Todd laughs. "What terms were they?"

"I explained to them that I am a student of life. I explained how all life is first and foremost metaphysical. The metaphysical precedes the physical. Just because we are not aware of this does not alter reality, but it does alter our relationship with reality. This becomes very apparent in crime and punishment. I asked how I could be expected to judge a person when I do not know their full history in relation to their crime against the supposed victim."

"What do you mean, supposed victim?" Bill asks.

"We are all immortal souls who constantly incarnate into new physical bodies. Let us take, for example, two men who are both passionate and have a tendency toward anger and violence. We will call them A and B. In one lifetime/incarnation and for whatever reason, A murders B. In the next incarnation the probability is strongly in favour of B murdering A. This goes on and on for several, or many, lifetimes. Generally, on a soul level they are attempting to find a solution, but on a physical level, with aggression and anger, the murders continue. So who is to blame? Who is the bad guy? Who is the victim? When I am suddenly asked to judge A or B for their crime against the other, how can I possibly do that? Of course, in the whole jury, I am the odd one out. I am the only person who sees that there is a bigger picture. Could I convince the other members of the jury that they are aware of only a single frame in the numberless frames of the continuing movie of A's and B's lives? I seriously doubt it. A truth out of timing!

"So I explain this in a simple and precise way by written letter to the jury selectors and I never hear from them again . . . until the next time!

Now, I no longer hear from them and I have no doubt that they consider me a nut case. And this is okay with me. Not having a truth understood is no problem, but for me to violate a truth that is in full timing for me, is to violate my own integrity. This, I do not do. Certainly not to be part of a jury of well-meaning people who are all profoundly ignorant of the deeper meaning of human life."

Bill shakes his head in wonder. "And putting aside major crimes and such like, this is all being played out in our daily lives, every one of us, on such a constant and mundane level that we have no awareness of it. Am I right? Is this what our everyday life is made up of?"

I nod. "Yes, Bill. You are correct. No human life is a new, fresh clean experience. Or if so, it is extremely rare. Life is the endless continuity of endless continuity. This is why people like me learn to see the bigger picture of life. In this way we can make the changes that lead to freedom."

"What is . . . real freedom?" Bill asks.

"Real freedom is when you are free to *freely* choose. When you have deep beliefs, when you are locked in a retribution program, when you are deeply religious, when you are dogmatic, when you have an inflexible mind, all these take away your ability to freely choose. If you are a devout Buddhist, you will make Buddhistic choices. A Catholic will make Catholic choices. A Muslim will make Muslim choices. And so it goes. There is no freedom within habit or dogma, because they will make old, well-used sameness choices. The fact that their choices may not work makes no difference at all. Habit and dogma are locked in. The place of freedom is when you are aware of, and live, within the movement of the moment. To be in that movement you have to be conscious. So for you to be conscious has to be a conscious choice. You could never subconsciously choose to be conscious, simply because this is impossible."

"Wow," Todd says, smiling. "I made a good choice with crime and punishment. I confess, I thought you might have nothing to say about it. As you speak, I am amazed at how you peel away my knowledge of life, revealing ever deeper layers that I have never even considered."

"I agree," Bill states emphatically. "As I attempt to listen and follow what you are saying, old concepts keep popping up . . . and they get annihilated. I get confused on whether to hold onto those old familiar concepts or to just let them go. All this makes my mind busy and I lose quite a bit of what you are sharing with us."

"Well," says Marsha, "you've just summed up the mental confusion I guess we're all going through. And emotional confusion too. I feel emotions coming and going all the time during, er . . . Michael's deeper discourses. Some are of sadness, others are of release and joy. It's all very confusing."

I smile at them. "As I have said, *just listen*. If you are *in* the moment with me, clarity will accompany you. If you are *out* of the moment, *evaluating* my words, then confusion will reign.

"Consider this, Bill, as an example of the everyday stuff. I touched upon this earlier, but by reiterating it with more detail, you should grasp it easier. You are driving your car and you have just stopped at the traffic lights. As you wait for the green light, a car runs into the back of you. You get out of your car to see what happened and realise that the back of your car is dented and that the woman driver is attempting to hide the lipstick that she was applying when she hit your car. What do you do? In our limited world, you exchange car and insurance details. You might decide to blame her and take her to court for damages. You would be perfectly within your rights."

Bill nods. "It would be within my rights, but I probably wouldn't."

I smile at him. "That's probably a good thing. I sometimes mention this scenario at an Intensive. Let's just say that across the road there is a coffee shop. Instead of swapping names, number plates and insurance, you ask the woman driver to follow you over to the coffee shop, and park over there. Once inside, you introduce yourself and tell her not to worry about such a trifling incident, and you buy her a cup of coffee."

"Gee . . . I *am* being a nice guy," Bill grins.

"Of course you are. It's intrinsic to your nature. So . . . you now ask her why she felt compelled to be careless and run into you, and you ask yourself why you felt that you should be in front of her so that she *could* run into you, and no one else. You tell her that it is fairly obvious that this is just another collision in many lives of collisions, and although they are minor collisions, if you go to court, it will take on a new complexion, getting nasty. She may think that you are crazy, and that's okay. You tell her that you hold no resentment and you bear no grudge, but of course, you need to truly *feel* this. You tell her that you choose to pay for yours and her damages, simply because you wish to end this cycle of collisions on a positive and loving energy. She may surprise you. She may fully understand you and admire and respect you for your decision. Either way, you have brought a beautiful conclusion to a long-term problem that was dogging both of you for more lifetimes than you might imagine."

"You know what . . . I think that's a wonderful way to look at life. To me – ever practical – you are saying, 'Act from the heart, rather than react from the wallet.' And I thank you for the suggestion. If such a thing happens, I'll do it. Or, of course, if the collision factor comes up in other ways."

I smile. "I like that. Act from the heart rather than react from the wallet. Very well said and very true on many, many occasions."

"So are we linked with all the people we incarnate with?" Marsha asks.

"Absolutely," I tell her. "All the aunts and uncles you had mutual dislike for, other relatives and friends you did not like, or reacted to, all incarnate in close proximity to each other both in linear time and location. Of course, the relationship roles are all reversed or otherwise changed, but it is still the same mental and emotional content in each person playing the same endless game of reaction and resentment. Reaction literally means re-enactment."

"Oh dear . . . I'm in trouble. I have several uncles I can't stand. They are all a bunch of sanctimonious bastards. So . . . what do I do?" she asks.

We all laugh. "In a nutshell . . . let go of all judgement and realise that they are emotional children, whatever age. Be kind to them in thoughts and actions and treat them in the way that you would like to be treated by them, but with no expectation of them showing any appreciation or changing in any way at all. It all comes from you. This will end the cycle for you."

"Really, I mean . . . truly? Wow! I could do that. I mean, it will take a bit of effort, but I can do it. Really, I mean as simple as that?" Marsha splutters.

"Truly, as simple as that. Simple it may be, but not easy. All you have to remember is not to be reactive. Be positive and loving and you have a clear home run! Goodbye to all the reactive negative reruns. Hello to newness!

"And now, so long as we have erred and strayed away from crime and punishment, we are ready for the next subject."

"Actually, we did not stray from crime and punishment," Marsha declares. "If, each time I react negatively to my relatives, I get to do it again in another lifetime . . . that truly is crime and punishment!"

I nod, chuckling. "Smart girl."

I realise, of course, that she is not really a girl, but when you get to my age, and increasingly so with every added year, most younger people seem to be more and more as boys and girls!

. . . SIXTEEN . . .

Intelligence and the Intellect

*The differences between intelligence and the intellect
are vast. We are Beings of conscious Intelligence.
While we live subconsciously we are dominated by the
intellect. Conscious intelligence is intrinsic to our very
Being, while the intellect is a tool of great potential, and
designed to be used as such.*

—Michael J. Roads

"I'M HOPING YOU CAN CHOOSE the next subject," Todd says. "I have a few
ideas, but I like it when you are on a roll. We have no defence against your
incisive words of wisdom, neither do we want any. You take us into places
that are very new and exciting, especially as we see the possibilities."

"Hmm . . . possibilities and probabilities is one possibility, but the
probability is that I will not choose them. Maybe another time," I mutter.
"Ah, one of my favourite topics is intelligence and the intellect. So be it."

"Aren't they pretty much the same?" Peter asks.

Hmm, so Peter is communicating again. I think the guys gave him a
strong talking to. He has been very subdued, but he is perking up more now.
I am glad that he is getting involved again. He is just a bit more entrenched

in his own opinions than the others, and more fearful of leaving their false safety and supposed security. But . . . he chose to come here!

"No, they are far from being the same." I tell him. "The intellect is intrinsic to the brain, while intelligence is all about the heart. Of course, your left-brain dominant colleagues would not agree with this. They would consider that intelligence is absolutely brain related.

"It seems to be completely overlooked that we are *holistic* Beings and, as such, we have the potential to use our body/mind/spirit in a far more holistic way than is currently happening. I have mentioned the hemispheres of the brain and our left-brain dominance. The ideal is to use our whole brain in perfect balance between the hemispheres, so that the whole mind will use and synchronise the brain hemispheres as is appropriate to the immediate moment. When we are able to do this, we live in a very different way.

"Among other things, I teach the way of the heart. Living heart first instead of head first. People go head first into trouble, never heart first. When we live with a focus of choosing Love, this literally, is intelligence in action. The intellect may question such a way of living, offering many negative scenarios of what could go wrong with this, but intelligence *knows*. When we develop to the point of having unconditional Love for self, the body goes through a huge energetic shift. This energy shift affects every cell in the body on a physical level. At this point, the heart naturally develops a coherent rhythm, rather than continuing with an incoherent one. This coherency allows the heart to send new, stronger energy carrying new information to the whole brain and they powerfully connect. When this happens, whole brain and heart in tandem energetically connect with the pineal. On a physical level the pineal gland is connected with the production of melatonin and serotonin. On a metaphysical level the pineal is the interface between the spirituality of the multiverse we live in and the holistic metaphysical Beings we are. Seen metaphysically, and depending on a person's spiritual development, the pineal activity appears as a halo around a person's head.

"With this connection in place, the person now has access to the wisdom of the ages, all held in the moment of now. This is the place of full human intelligence and ultimately the place of genius. Genius has almost nothing to do with the isolated left-brain's cleverness. I have already said this, but we see so many examples of intellectual cleverness that are profoundly stupid. Our whole political system is a good example. The actual difference between intelligence and the intellect is vast. We *are* Beings of conscious Intelligence. While we live subconsciously we are dominated by the intellect. Conscious intelligence is who we are. The intellect is a tool of great potential. When our mortal body dies, our intellect experiences a form of degradation, but we continue with our intelligence undisturbed and uninterrupted. Of course, it helps greatly if we ever use it. Most people don't!"

Peter stares at me, white-faced, expressionless.

"You are fairly challenged right now because you are an intellectual man," I say to him. "But I am not in any way reducing your status. Only you can do that! You have grown up with a common belief in the IQ tests as a standard of measuring our intelligence. I'm telling you that they are a joke, intellectual rubbish. Consciousness cannot be separated from intelligence, nor can intelligence be separated from consciousness. They are One. You, or anyone, can use as much intelligence as you choose, with one proviso: you must be conscious. You cannot subconsciously use intelligence. You can subconsciously use the intellect, but not intelligence. And if you look at the world we live in, or watch the world news on TV, you will see clear affirmation of this on a daily basis. Human intelligence is a virtual stranger on this planet."

"It's very sobering to learn that we, as a species, are so . . . er, very undeveloped. Here was me thinking that sure, we had a few problems, but as I listen to you, I am overwhelmed by the magnitude of our sheer ignorance, of our inadequacies," Bill states. "Could you be wrong about all this?"

I laugh. "You remind me of myself many years ago. I was in my early thirty's and my late wife and I had been given a couple of books to read. They were written by a bit of a mystery man, Lobsang Rampa. He claimed to be a Tibetan monk, although this was disputed, not that it matters. Anyway, one book was titled *The Hermit,* and the other, *The Third Eye.* We devoured them both and they rang loud, chiming bells in our hearts. When we were finished, my wife said to me, 'Dare we believe this?' I said to her, 'If he's right, then there are a heck of a lot of people who are wrong.

Could he be wrong?' We went back and forth on this, until finally we both declared, 'I'm going to trust my heart and accept this.' The whole course of our lives changed in that moment. We never looked back. As, to the best of our ability, we lived what we learned, so we progressed along our path toward a greater Truth. So you will understand why asking me if I could be wrong makes me smile!"

I chuckle. "I guess since then my books have launched many other people onto their path. I certainly hope so. I consider it a great honour."

I meet Bill's eyes. "No, I am not wrong about life. But this is not *for me* to decide *for you*. Back to timing. *You* have to make that decision." I smile at him. "And you've already made it. Your heart knows, for that's where the intelligence is. When people question if they are ready for an Intensive, I usually tell them that all they need is an open heart and an open mind."

"Your clarity and certainty are very reassuring," Anita says. "I have felt doubts arise, but you are so sure of yourself it is a compelling energy."

"Again, this is only because you are here in right timing. If you were not, my energy would be far more threatening to you, more as though I were trying to force you to agree with me. But that is not happening. You have full freedom to accept or reject my words. When you all arrived here and we met, energetically I felt that there would be accord between us. I felt the possibility of Peter's struggle, and I accepted this. Every group, large or small, has its own unique dynamic and Peter is part of this. It's perfect."

Peter looks at me quizzically. "Do you mean perfect, or just okay?"

"I mean perfect. Everything is perfect when you see the bigger picture. Chaos in humanity is where intelligence is disconnected from aware human consciousness. It's perfect. Why? Because in the chaos is the opportunity to find that connection and embrace it. Result; no more chaos in your life. There will probably be chaos all around you, but this is because other people also have to make the quantum leap that you just made. You cannot do this for them and neither can I do this for you. Let me make the point that the clarity and certainty in my life are very *enabling*. Most people are *disabled* by doubt, scepticism and cynicism. I challenge that aspect in some people."

...SEVENTEEN...

Possibilities and Probabilities

I'm saying that where you focus, energy flows. So when you consider the probability factor of a repeating pattern of a problematic behaviour, then obviously the last thing you should do is maintain a focus on that problem.

Problems feed on energy, the same as we do. If you refuse to feed the problematic behaviour with energy, it dwindles and fades. Instead of attempting to correct the problem, you focus on the attributes and abilities of the person you are counselling.

—Michael J. Roads

"THIS ALL LEADS US IN PERFECT TIMING to the beachfront of possibilities and probabilities," I say beaming at them. "I just knew we would get there!"

"I honestly don't see how," Anita replies, laughing.

"Well, the possibilities are quite strong that all humanity could just suddenly begin using far more intelligence, but the far stronger probability is that it won't happen anytime soon," I tell her.

Bill has his shrewd look again. "So while all things are possible, that by no means suggests that they are probable," he says.

"Very good, Bill. That's the way of it. Let me explain what I call the Probability Factor to you. When I was a teenager, I used a .22 rifle. I became a very good shot, as they say. If I aimed at a reasonably distant target, the probability is that the bullet would hit it. It is very highly improbable that the bullet would go halfway, then turn at right angles to miss the target. So the Probability Factor says the bullet will go in the direction to which it was aimed. The possibility exists that by some fluke the bullet could be deflected and thus turn at a right angle, but it is highly improbable that this would happen."

"So what relationship does any of this have with our ongoing current discussions?" Bill asks, in a slightly exasperated tone.

I smile at him. "Okay, the probability is that one of your parents was rather impatient with you. Possibly your father. Am I correct?"

Bill regards me with astonishment. "How in the world did you figure that out? Yes, my father was *very* impatient with me."

"And you really didn't like it, did you?"

"No, I felt that he was mocking me. I hated it."

"And as you got older, he was particularly impatient if you made a remark that seemed irrelevant to your discussion," I suggested.

"Incredible . . . but yes. But how could you possibly know that?"

"Simply because you unknowingly exhibited the same impatience with me when you asked what relationship possibilities and probabilities have with our current discussions," I reply. "So I will tell you. The probability is that many of the personality traits of your father that you did not like are in your daily repertoire of personality traits to this day. As you just demonstrated. In fact, you said that you hated it. This implies that the more strongly it affected your emotions, the more probable it is that you will carry it forward into your own life. And, I repeat once more, all unknowingly and unwittingly."

Bill looks a bit shaken. "My mother has often told me that I am my father all over again, but I dismissed her words as nonsense. Why would I copy a man that I did not particularly like as I grew older? In fact, I've tried to be the very opposite of him. Obviously . . . I've failed."

I put a hand on his shoulder and squeeze. "It's okay. I can tell you how to deal with it and make the changes you want."

He looks at me hopefully. "Do you think that's possible?" he asks.

I smile. "Very possible, and in all probability, yes, I do.

"First of all, answer a question. As a man married to Mary, if I remember correctly, do you ever find yourself impatient with her?"

He sighs. "Yes . . . all too often."

"Does she know your father?"

"They met a few times, but we live a long way away from my parents, so we seldom see them nowadays. More of an annual event."

"Okay. The way I see it is that emotionally you are still very involved with your father. You think about the way that he used to demean you, even though you probably don't talk about it. So, energetically, you bring the past forward into the present. Where you focus, your energy flows, so if he is in your focus and your energy flows toward the habits that you didn't like, then unrealised, you repeat them. And the probability is that this will continue."

Bill stares at me bleakly. "I thought you said you could help!"

"I can, but I need you to fully realise that *you cannot change and remain the same*. Do you get that?"

He grins hopefully, nodding.

"This is what you do. You begin by having a full-on relationship with yourself. You learn to fully appreciate everything about you that you like. You ask your wife and a close friend to write a list of all that they most appreciate in you, and you learn to appreciate in yourself all that they appreciate in you. And, of course, you put your father out of your emotional and mental life. You learn to relate to the people living in your life on a daily basis, not to people who are memories in the past."

"And what do I do about my father obsession?"

"You focus on everything in yourself that you enjoy. Every other aspect of yourself that you don't like, you totally ignore. You don't attempt to correct any disliked obsession, you simply ignore it. What you ignore withers away from lack of energy. What you attempt to correct thrives on the energy. And it does not go away. It truly is that simple!"

He nods thoughtfully. "That's exactly the *reverse* of what I have been doing. And what I've been doing doesn't work."

I nod. "It's a bit painful when you consider how many people are taught ways to heal emotional problems that go against all the principles of Truth. And, of course, they don't work. They may appear to be working for you on a short term basis, but eventually this will break down and the old habit will be reestablished. It's a common occurrence."

Bill rolls his eyes. "Tell me about it. As I listen to you, I realise that we are guilty of this as counsellors ourselves. We were taught how to counsel people and we follow our practice and code fairly carefully. Sometimes it seems to be working very well, then it suddenly falls apart and the person is back where they started."

"Candles in the dark!"

"So you are saying that we should not focus on . . . er . . . I'm lost!"

I chuckle. "I'm saying that where you focus, energy flows. So when you consider the probability factor of a repeating pattern of a problematic behaviour, then obviously the last thing you should do is maintain a focus on that problem. Problems feed on energy, the same as we do. If you refuse to feed the problematic behaviour with energy, it dwindles and fades. Instead of attempting to correct the problem, you focus on the attributes and abilities of the person you are counselling. You teach them self-appreciation. In this way you and they are feeding energy to their *higher* qualities. Sometimes it will even draw skills to the surface that, unrealised, were developed in a past lifetime."

Bill gives me a sceptical look. "You're kidding me . . . surely?"

I shake my head. "Truly. You are looking at a perfect example of this. I remember long ago, as a farmer, going to a beef conference. At the end we were invited to ask questions. I had one that was important to me, so I raised my hand in the suggested way. Then, a man with a microphone made his slow way among the farmers as one by one their questions were addressed. By the time he reached me, I was a sweating, trembling, nervous wreck . . . all just to ask a question. He gave me the mike, and all I managed was a strangled squawk, then I shoved the mike back into his hand, cringing as many of the nearby farmers laughed."

Bill looks very sympathetic.

I chuckle. "If a farmer had then told me, 'Don't worry, one day you will be public speaking all over the world', I would have recommended immediate psychiatric treatment for him! And yet, this is what happened.

Only a few years later, I found skills of communication that in timing, came bubbling to the surface. Much later on my spiritual path I learned that I had been a wandering heretic at some stage in a few past lives, and that I was very well versed with speaking in public . . . albeit often to a seriously unfriendly audience!"

"So the conference was out of your timing, but a year or so later the timing arrived?" Bill asks for confirmation.

I nod. "Actually, quite a few years later. We are our own timing in every aspect of our lives."

EIGHTEEN

Emotional Attachments – Emotional Balance

If you have no attachments to an opinion or an outcome, you will find that you seldom ever get angry. If you have no attachments to what other people think of you, good or bad, you have the foundations of inner peace. If you have no attachments to your own opinion, when other people disagree with you, there will be no emotional reactions, no anger. This is a path toward emotional balance.

—Michael J. Roads

CAROLYN COMES WALKING INTO THE ROOM and busies herself taking plates and loaded dishes from the kitchen server and placing them on the dining table on the deck. She is fast and efficient.

"Okay people, I have made a large bowl of salad and a couple of quiches. One vegetarian and one non-vegetarian. Your plates are on the table, all is ready, so now is a good time to eat and relax."

She smiles at them all warmly. "I'm sure your brains are buzzing with this mini-seminar you are getting. Michael is a bit intense when he gets going, and from what I have heard, he is *definitely* going very well!"

She looks from one to another. "If anyone wants more hot tea or coffee, it is on the table. I can also bring out iced tea with fresh mint and honey if anyone would prefer it. So . . . eat, drink and enjoy."

With the day getting progressively warmer, she quickly has orders for her iced-mint tea speciality.

I think of asking Carolyn to stay and join in with our discussions, but I know that she will decline as she is catching up on office work. She always is! Uninterrupted time in the office is valuable to Carolyn, with the ever-constant emails and suchlike. While we both have endless enthusiasm for what we do, I consider that she is the organisational brains of the outfit, while I am the mouth that could continue to talk under a tonne of wet cement!

For about fifteen minutes we all eat in silence, then, having finished my lunch, I decide that I will talk while they continue eating. Listening and eating are very compatible!

"During the morning, as I have been chatting with you, I noticed that several times one or more of you became quite emotional."

I quickly hold my hands up in a peace gesture. "Not that there is anything wrong in being emotional. I consider myself an emotional man. But this brings me to another topic that involves everyone. And that is our next point of discussion . . . emotional balance. When I say this involves everyone, I do not mean that all people are emotionally balanced, far from it. I mean that not only are we a very emotional species, but that the majority of people are quite seriously emotionally inadequate."

Looking at their faces, I can see that my statement is challenging. I smile at them. "I am not saying that any of *you* are emotionally inadequate, but your energy via your body language is clearly stating exactly that. What I am saying is pressing the emotional buttons of three of you."

I suppress a grin as I pause, watching them looking at each other.

"Oh, come on . . . we are all friends, right? So Todd is comfortable with my statement and, somewhat to my surprise, so is Anita. The rest of you are going through various expressions of personal embarrassment. Why? Bill, what's the problem? Peter, why are you are looking so angry again? Marsha, what gives in your emotional world?"

I give them a big, friendly enquiring smile as the three of them scowl back at me. They definitely do not like the personal treatment.

"I'm very aware that I'm an emotional mess," Marsha says, with a sigh. "And that it makes my counselling work far more difficult. I do my best to hide it from people, and because I'm aware of my inadequacy I rather successfully compensate for it."

"Well, good for you," I say to her. Then I look at Bill and Peter.

"Personally, I fail to see that it is any of your business," Peter declares.I grin. "Fair enough, it isn't."

"I too am aware of my emotional problem," Bill states. "I know that it comes from my old relationship with my father, so as I take on board your earlier suggestions, I'm pretty sure that it will help me emotionally."

"I agree, I also think it will if you *live* it," I say, encouragingly.

"Okay, I have mentioned emotions several times during the morning. If you remember, we have the low emotions, the midway emotions and the high emotions. Sadly, most people are emotionally stuck between low and midway, which is not to their advantage."

"And why is that?" Peter asks, aggressively.

I can hear the suppressed anger struggling in his voice.

"Because this is the place of emotional reaction. You are reacting to me in this very moment. You are angry with me for provoking you, but you are far angrier with yourself for being so easily provoked by someone whom you know is not actually trying to provoke you at all. This, Peter, is the nasty stewpot of emotional turmoil, of emotional inadequacy."

Peter swallows, taking a deep, shuddering breath. "You are exactly right. I am so angry with myself . . . and I have been for so long. I need it to end." He slumps his shoulders, almost pleading. "How do I do this?"

I reach out to him and gently squeeze his shoulder. "Peter, I am not a counsellor. I do counsel people, but more as a wise man than a counsellor; more as a spiritual teacher than a counsellor. I don't know the clever modern techniques of emotional counselling, or any counselling: all I know is Truth. However, if you are willing, I can suggest a way that will gradually bring balance to your emotions, and this works. Balanced emotions are not up and down, excited one moment depressed the next; they are more steadfast, far less erratic. Well-balanced emotions are the ideal."

Peter looks anxious. "Is this something I have to learn intellectually, or is it something I have to do?"

I smile at him. "First of all remember this, and do your best to live it. I learned this from Carolyn: *Taking offence is no different from giving offence.* Many people are offensive; they give it and take it, living in an ever ongoing series of emotional reactions. Quite often you have taken offence from something I said, but not once have I been deliberately offensive. I don't do such things. When you cut this 'offence-defence' cycle out of your daily life, you will be considerably more emotionally relaxed. And this is good. This sounds very little, but from this little comes muchness!"

I look into his eyes. "You asked if this was something you need to learn intellectually, but it is not. Most of the time emotions do not make any sense at all, yet people try to intellectually understand them. What is the point of this? Emotions seldom make sense . . . they are emotions! Laughing at a funeral is not uncommon, or crying at a wedding. Confused emotions. Some men can't cry, and laugh hysterically when they don't mean to. Emotional turmoil. All this is common, everyday stuff. So what I am saying is, let emotions be emotions without being heavily suppressed, or analysed."

"What about my anger?" Peter asks.

I nod. "Yes, not a good idea to suppress it, not a good idea to express it. So what to do with it? So, Peter, think about this very carefully. What can make you angry if you have no attachment to an opinion and no attachment to an outcome?"

He opens his mouth to quickly answer several times, then closes it. A puzzled expression gradually spreads over his face and he visibly relaxes. A little smile tugs at one corner of his mouth. "This sounds crazy, but . . . I can't think of a single thing."

I nod again, noting that the others are riveted by our conversation.

"Correct. If you have no attachments to an opinion or an outcome, you will find that you seldom, if ever, get angry. If you have no attachments to what other people think of you, good or bad, you have the foundations of inner peace. If you have no attachments to your own opinion, when other people disagree with you, there will be no emotional reactions, no anger. No trying to convince them that you are right! It is so peaceful living this way. This is a path toward emotional balance."

"What about the way that elephants are being slaughtered for ivory or the massive deforestation that is happening in the world?" Anita puts in. "Doesn't all this senseless destruction make you angry?

"I understand your point, of course. But how would my getting emotional over this be of any value to the forests or the elephants? I sign many petitions to help prevent these terrible things and I give money toward it, but I do not get emotional over it. To me, child pornography and pedophiles are far worse, but it happens and always has. Where I focus, my energy flows. I refuse to give any of my energy to such debased corruption. I help counteract it by teaching people how to live in a higher state of consciousness. I help counteract it by teaching people how to choose Love. I help counteract it by refusing to lower my own consciousness to the lower energy of those sick and corrupted people."

Anita looks contrite. "I wish I had that higher consciousness."

"To return to what I was saying. Anger is an effect, not a cause. Can any of you explain to me the intelligence behind anger management? I repeat, anger is an effect, not a cause. Why manage it? Why create it to manage? We are a species going insane! All you have to do is remove the cause. And the cause of anger is emotional attachments to our opinions, to being right, and to our wanted and/or expected outcomes. I have let go of those pointless attachments and I do not get angry. Once in twenty years . . . and I won't do that again. Why? Because anger kills angry people – self killing self – and if that is not stupid enough, angry people kill other people too. What a complete waste of energy, creating cycles of pain and suffering. Like I said, we are a species attempting to manage our insanity. And we will fail. All you have to do is make conscious choices that honour you, and there is nothing honouring within anger. And, of course, you are required to consciously live those conscious choices. I recommend choosing Love!"

Suddenly standing up to his full height and looming over me, Peter clumsily attempts to embrace me. Something he is clearly unused to doing.

"Let me get up, it makes hugging easier," I say, surging to my feet.

He still looms over me as we share an awkward, but heartfelt hug.

When he sits down, he gives me an embarrassed smile. "I'm really sorry that I've been so rude and difficult. Listening to you was rather like having my teeth extracted with no sedation. I was numb, but I felt the deep,

101

stabbing pain of your Truth."

He looks at Todd and Bill. "And thank you guys for not letting me run away when that is all I wanted to do. When you told me to take your car, Todd, and go . . . I knew that I should not, that I could not, that I dare not. I knew that I would never get another chance like this. So, thank you all for your patience and tolerance with me."

Bill catches my eye and smiles in delight. He obviously likes Peter, and is clearly a good friend to him.

NINETEEN

Inner Harmony and Surrender

You surrender the questions, you surrender the need to
save the world, you surrender the need for a purpose, you
surrender searching. You finally surrender. You let go.
You allow. You allow yourself to be fully yourself with no
pressure, no should or shouldn't, no can or can't . . . you
simply relax. But let me be very clear, this relaxation is
not inertia, it is not inactivity, it is a truly dynamic-living
state of consciousness.

—Michael J. Roads

"I IMAGINE THAT YOUR LIFE has been one of resistance," I say to Peter.

He looks at me quizzically. "How do you mean?"

"I mean resisting the path of your father, resisting your spontaneity, your deeper impulses and resisting life in general as you plotted your own path in life. By contrast, you could allow life to express itself through you, but you chose to imprint your personal expression into life. That sort of thing."

He smiles at me. "Finally I can comfortably say that I have no clear idea of what you are talking about. But yes, I consider that I have plotted my own path in life and I made sure that it did not deviate into wasted time and other distractions. Is this what you mean?"

I nod. "Yes. And this is okay, but my question is; do you honestly know where you are going in life as you create this path?"

He looks sad. "I did . . . until today. Now I realise that my path is all about financial security and that it is fear based. I really thought it was a path toward success and fulfilment. I often wondered why I was so unhappy."

"Let me be clear, this is not a wrong or bad path, but it *is* a path that takes you ever deeper into fear, into the illusions of life. This is why you are unhappy. There is no Truth in such a path," I tell him.

Peter is now far more receptive and open. He is doing very well.

"So how would you suggest I create my life path?" he asks.

I shake my head. "I'm not going to suggest how you should live at all. Discovering your path is part of your own empowerment process. However, I will tell you the way I do it. First, I trust myself fully because I unconditionally Love myself. Love and trust is a super-powerful combination. With this in place, I have surrendered to life. I allow life to live me, rather than me live life. I have no resistance to the ebb and flow of life, no struggle to go *my* way. I have learned that every way is my way when I am in harmony with life. And this is the key; to find that place of inner harmony.

"If we are out of harmony with self, we are out of harmony with life. We then struggle with life, falling into the pit of blame. We blame governments, we blame other people, whoever, whatever . . . we blame. But *we* are the creators of our lives! No one else can create our lives. Blame does not work, yet people waste lifetimes lost in blame. I call it the blame game. Pointless! "The reality is that people living in the illusion plot their path in life, doing their best to ensure that it is based in financial security and success. When you fully embrace your spirituality, your Oneness with life, this all changes. You are now faced with the reality of wondering *what is my path? Is there a path for me? What is my purpose in life?*

"These, and other questions, will take you on many a wild-goose chase, until finally you reach the end of this process. Looking to fulfil your purpose takes some people lifetimes. Finally, if you stay with it, you surrender the questions, you surrender the need to save the world, you surrender the need for a purpose, you surrender searching. You finally surrender. You let go. You allow. You allow yourself to be fully yourself with no pressure, no should or shouldn't, no can or can't . . . you simply relax. But let me be very clear, this relaxation is not inertia, it is not inactivity, it is a truly dynamic-living state of consciousness."

I pause, regarding my audience.

Marsha sighs heavily. "I can follow you, just, but I also got lost in my 'if only' thoughts. If only I could live like that, if only it was possible for me."

"Do you seriously think that I would waste my time teaching people a way to live if I thought it was impossible for them? Of course you can live like this. It is your destiny. It is everyone's destiny. But the *timeframe* is your own choice. Most people never make this choice, but *not* choosing is the choice of self-denial. So you cannot *not* choose! Better to clearly choose and, to the best of your ability, live your choice. Of course, you can take as long as you wish, lifetimes, centuries, aeons, or, like me, you can give it your full focus and literally move mountains. And to clarify this, those *metaphoric* mountains are made of blame and doubt, of insecurity and illusions, and they are indeed, massive – almost, but not quite, unmovable – mountains!"

Marsha looks at me earnestly. "No, I don't think that you would waste your time teaching the impossible, not for a moment. I guess I'm revealing my doubt about myself . . . to me! I always kept my self-doubt tucked away out of sight, so I could forget about it. I guess I hoped it would go away."

I nod. "Self-doubt is self-created. It indicates to me that you are fairly critical of yourself. If someone else was to criticise you all day and every day, would you spend much time with them? No, you would avoid them. But you cannot avoid yourself. So, dear girl, please stop criticising yourself and replace it with self-*appreciation*. As you do this, self-doubt will gradually fade away – as you hoped for – and self-confidence will gradually grow. And it will all be down to you changing from what does *not* work for you . . . to what *does* work for you! As I keep saying . . . *you* are the creator of your life!"

"You talk about surrender. It takes a lot of courage to just surrender to life," Todd says. "I'm not quite sure that I understand. What do you surrender to? What prevents you from drifting along aimlessly in life?"

I chuckle. "Actually it requires a lot of courage to live a spiritual way of life. Much of what you do will not be understood by you, or by most other people." I smile. "But a spiritual teacher would understand!

"Okay, so you surrender your personal program, or your personal path, to the soul who you are. You let go of the dominant left-brain drive toward success and you allow the feeling/intuition that arises from your heart to determine the new way that you will live. And to be serious, this *does* require a lot of courage. It will frighten you. Your thoughts will rebel against you. You will find this way of life irrational and illogical, and you will not be able to justify it to your family or friends. However, if you continue with this, and you go through the inner turmoil that it will create, steadfastly listening to the whispers of your heart while ignoring the screaming of your brain, you will eventually come to a new place of inner harmony. You will find a place of inner peace."

I look at Todd. "Are you with me?"

He nods.

"From this platform of inner peace and harmony, your new life will unfold itself like the eternal lotus flower unfolding its petals. And you trust. You now trust yourself, you trust life. When you are heart-centred and connected to life from the heart, you will one day find the inner space of unfathomable joy. Your life will be a dance, and only you and Love will hear the music to which you dance, for the music will be of your creation."

Todd looks at me incredulously. "Really? I mean are you seriously saying that all this can come from surrendering your path in life to . . . er, the stirrings in your heart. Let's say I believe you . . . and I do, but how long is the process that a person has to go through to reach this? I mean, with the inner turmoil, the doubts, the fears, all that . . . before reaching the inner peace?"

I nod at him sympathetically. "That, my friend, depends entirely on the person involved. Let me give you a metaphor. Consider you are asking me how long it will take on a train ride to reach Sydney. My answer will be that the duration of the ride depends entirely on which station you get on the train. Some people will be more spiritually advanced than others, so it will take them less time. Others will be more fearful and doubting, so it will take longer. A few, regardless of their spiritual status, will more quickly surrender to the process and progress rapidly. In other words, it all depends on each person."

"Could you give me some clue?" he pleads, smiling.

I sigh. Everybody wants an instant fix. "Possibly a few months, but in all probability quite a few years."

Todd nods. "And you cannot force surrender, can you?"

I shake my head. "No, you cannot force it. But let me say this; the more conscious you are, the faster the process will proceed. Being conscious will make a big difference. Staying subconscious will delay the timing and make the whole process more frightening and difficult. In fact, I would go as far as to say that if you think you cannot do this, you are right. But equally, if you think you *can* do this, I agree with you, you are right."

"So it's all about timing, yes?" Todd asks.

I nod. "Once again, it is all about timing. However, as I continue to say, *you* are the timing of your Truth. You, and you only, determine when you are ready to make the quantum leap in consciousness. But, eventually, no matter how long it takes, that incredible leap will have to be made by every single human Being."

TWENTY

Prayer and Religion

An old priest said, 'Speak to us of religion.' And he
answered saying: *If you should enter the temple for
no other purpose than asking you shall not receive.
And if you enter the temple to humble yourself you
shall not be lifted; or should you enter into it to beg
for the good of others you shall not be heard.
It is enough that you enter the temple invisible.*
—Kahlil Gibran

FOR A WHILE THERE IS SILENCE AMONG US. A kookaburra in a nearby tree
seems to think that he has some message for us, screaming his hysterical,
weird, laughing cry. Ignoring him, my five guests are engrossed in finishing
their salad and quiche. I smile. Hmm, maybe I was wrong, and you cannot
eat and listen . . . effectively!

Anita looks at me pensively. "Okay, how about something completely
different," she says. "How about your views on religion and prayer? You
seem to be controversial on every subject, how about this one?"

I laugh. "Me? . . . controversial! From my perspective I am the one with a
Truth that is in harmony with all natural life. I am appropriate to the times.

Today's 'normality' is controversial, ridiculous, heading toward insanity, and completely inappropriate. 'Normality' today is radically opposed to life, while my reality is quintessential to life. Seriously, do you think it is likely that I would see eye to eye with religion? Why? Do you come from a religious family? What prompted this?"

"Yes, my parents are very religious. But to be fair, although I had to do the church routine when I was young, they were not extreme in any way, nor did they attempt to force me toward religion," Anita replies.

I nod. "And were any of your grandparents religious?"

"Yes, my dad's parents. And strict, and extreme. That's why my dad was so strongly against pushing religion onto his children. We all made our own choices as we moved into our mid-teens. My older sister stayed with it, I did not. Somehow, religion did not sit right with me."

"Christians? What denomination?" I ask.

She smiles. "Methodists. Quite reasonable compared with some!"

I nod. "A while ago on my Facebook page, a statement appeared. I have no idea who takes credit for it, but it was very astute. 'Your spirituality is your relationship with the divine. Religion is crowd control.' I suspect it was meant to be humorous, but it is so very true. There are many religions in the world, and I am unfamiliar with most of them. As an outsider, looking in, many of them seem to share certain characteristics; with regard to prayer, they place an intermediary between you and God. In a world of Oneness, this is either profound ignorance, where the religion knows nothing of Truth, or it is profoundly stupid. We are not separate from God. Or, and this is my view of it, religion is a means of controlling people through a created fear of God.

"I was raised as a Christian, in the Church of England. So this was the foundation on which I was supposed to build my spiritual life. My history may be a bit rusty, but I am aware that during the reign of Henry VIII, the Catholic Church had more power over the people than the King of England. 'Not good', says Henry, 'very undesirable.' So Henry established the Church of England, which was very *non*-Catholic. And, of course, he made himself the head of the church, along with all his ruthless sexual ambitions. Smart! This move was so successful that within a hundred years or so you would be very unwise to let it be known that you were a Catholic.

We can smile at this today, yet this sad and sick energetic foundation of the past has given birth to all the sickening and nefarious sexual activity of so many of the priests in the various Christian religions. Those people who, like myself, were born into the Church of England, have a sorry spiritual platform based in one ruthless man's ambition. Not exactly the right energy for spiritual development!"

"Wow," Anita replies. "I didn't know that. So how did you move away from the church's influence? What prompted you?"

I chuckle. "I was about thirty-five when I was hit shockingly hard by a question out of the blue: Who am I? I had no idea, no clue. But this was the very beginning of my spiritual path and it took me firmly away from religion. To be clear, I have nothing against religion. If people want to be led and manipulated and thus reduced, that is their choice. I want no part of it. And to be honest, I have little sympathy for those who act like sheep, willing to be led into a religious delusion which actually leads them toward spiritual decay.

"I was counselling a man about his spirituality and his religion. He was raised as a Catholic, and was struggling to leave Catholicism and the local church. He told me he was literally threatened with eternal damnation if he did. Incredible! Another man in a similar discussion told me that he was struggling between his Catholic faith and his new spiritual path. I asked him why he still went to church. He told me it was so he could pray to Mother Mary. I asked him what he prayed for, and to my surprise he told me that he reads from a list of things that he wants Mother Mary to deliver into his life. When I asked him if he ever simply prayed to share his Love and devotion with Mother Mary, he told me that such an idea had never occurred to him."

Todd laughs. "You obviously are not impressed by religions."

I shake my head. "It isn't that simple. When I am in Japan each year I visit many of their Buddhist and Shinto temples. Some of the temples are miles away from easy reach, yet each day a stream of people makes its way over rocks and through forests to these remote temples to pray. I have no idea what they pray for or about, but if a Christian church was located in such a place, it would be utterly deserted. I have a metaphysical friend who is a Japanese god. He/it is a god of the human heart. This god told me that today, in Japan, most prayers are based in want. Long ago they were based in devotion. We are all the poorer for this. And, just to finish this aspect, the Japanese gods whom I have met all focus toward a Supreme Creator."

"But there is only one God," Peter protests.

"Thank you, Peter, this reminds me of an aspect of our religion that I may have overlooked; Christian arrogance. I have no doubt that you were raised a Christian."

He nods, frowning.

"I, too, had this unwitting arrogance. I also grew up believing that there is only one God. We Christians were right; all other religions who disagreed with us were wrong. What breathtaking arrogance. India has hundreds, maybe thousands of gods and goddesses, but my Christian belief dismissed them all. We were right, so they must be wrong. All the other non-Christian religions and the cultures that grew around them were deluded. Until, in a metaphysical journey, I met two Japanese gods and a goddess. Happily they educated me into a broader view of life. Today, my relationship with God has completely changed."

"In what way?" Anita asks.

I scratch my head. "Hmm . . . I'm not sure that this is the appropriate timing." Then I made my decision. "Okay, as a child I was taught that God created man in his image. I have learned that this is false. The truth is that man created God in *his* image. This is all about religious control of the masses. If you maintain a convincing lie for long enough it eventually becomes acceptable. If, over centuries, you continue to perpetuate and perpetrate the lie it becomes a common 'truth'. Eventually, a sadly ignorant humanity concretised it into such a rigid belief that, no matter how false, it has now become a 'fact' . . . while remaining false.

"However, the gods taught me that there is a divine state of Supreme Creation. This is neither a singularity – like the God created by man – nor is it a duality, nor is it a collective. This Supreme Creation – which is never-ending creation – is a state of conscious intelligence so far beyond human comprehension that it is way, way out of timing for human Truth. This is why I hesitate to speak of it."

"But how can you know this if it is out of human timing?" Peter asks.

"I have nothing further to say on the matter."

Anita gives me a winning grin. "I don't disbelieve you. But where does this Supreme Creation reside? I mean . . . where is it?"

"Eternity," I reply.

... TWENTY-ONE ...

A Metaphysical World

Metaphysical journeying is not something that you practice
with an achievement orientation; it is a basic human
potential that awaits when your relationship with life has
undergone a profound change. When you are truly in the
state of consciousness of knowing that you are an immortal,
metaphysical Being, and that you are not a physical body,
then this mystical potential rises to the surface of your
awareness ... if it is in right timing and is appropriate for you.
—Michael J. Roads

"But what exactly *is* eternity?" she persists.

I laugh. "Good one. Eternity is eternal, infinite. Linear time is a human construct. If you allow the soul-Self you are to leave the physical body, and leave all the endless constructs of the mind, then, maybe ... eternity!"

"That doesn't make sense," Anita objects.

I nod. "Correct. Eternity is an experience way beyond our sense or senses. Even sense has to be left behind, along with the intellect and all its multitude of confining beliefs. We are talking about pure metaphysics."

"What exactly is metaphysics? You have used the term metaphysical many times and I've been intending to ask," Todd says.

"First and foremost, metaphysical means beyond the physical. In other words all metaphysical reality is non-physical. Everything on a slower energy frequency than the speed of light, we can see. It is physical. When the energy frequency is faster than the speed of light, we do not see it. It is metaphysical.

"As I have mentioned a number of times, we are not the physical beings that we see in a mirror. We are not bodies clothed in flesh. We are Beings of pure energy on a very high frequency. We, each and every one of us, are immortal, metaphysical Beings. Primarily, we live in a metaphysical world. This indicates that the metaphysical *precedes* the physical. We have lost the awareness of our immortality, we have lost our metaphysical connection with Self and we have lost our metaphysical connection with Nature. We are basically a species lost in deep illusion. When you look at a tree, or a forest, you believe that it is physical because as a physical person you relate *only* to a physical world. But this is not how it is. A greater reality exists. In this greater reality the tree is the physical reflection from a greater metaphysical reality. A tree is metaphysical energy, like we are, and like us it also has a physical expression. But this is the *least* of the tree, compared with its evolving immortal energetic expression. The idea that a tree is purely physical creates false beliefs based in illusion.

"However, now is not the time to explain all this. It is a huge and rather complex subject. As I was saying moments ago, the metaphysical precedes the physical. In other words, thoughts precede actions. I know we believe that we can act without thought, but thoughts are there on a subconscious level, genuinely unnoticed. Thoughts also precede emotions, and that, too, is mostly unrealised. Our every health issue first energetically affects our metaphysical energy body, but our normal medical practices stay firmly with treatment for our physical bodies only. There are healers like John of God in Brazil, and others of a similar ilk around the world, who work with the metaphysical body, all healing people in a way that Western medical science cannot accept."

"I have read enough of your books to know that you often travel metaphysically," Todd says. "How do you actually do this? Could I do it? Could any normal person do this?"

I laugh aloud. "Define normal."

Todd shakes his head, laughing. "Okay, point taken. But could I do it?"

Still chuckling, I reply, "I consider that you are not quite normal. Do *you* think that metaphysical journeying is possible for you?"

Todd looks pensive. "I like the idea very much."

I smile. "Fair enough. But you have to realise that no 'normal' person is going to even consider leaving their body until death does them part! And if you were truly 'normal' you probably would not read my books, unless, of course, you wanted to leave normality! Nor would you be here talking with me. So maybe you are beyond normality enough to be able to metaphysically journey."

"Will you tell me . . . us, how?" Todd asks.

"Yes, please. I've also read a bit about your journeys and would like such a skill," Anita pleads.

With just a hint of hesitation, the other three nod.

Hmm, looks like we have our next topic. They all think that this is a skill to master, but it is not quite so simple. First, it is a state of consciousness to reach, *then* a skill to master. I explain this to them.

"How do we do the required growing in consciousness?" Anita asks.

I shake my head. "You are all approaching this in the way that a hopeful swimmer would train for the Olympics. This is not something that you practice for with an achievement orientation; this is a basic human potential that awaits when your relationship with life has undergone a profound change. When you are truly in the state of consciousness of *knowing* that you are an immortal, metaphysical Being and that you are not a physical body, then this mystical potential rises to the surface of your awareness . . . if it is in right timing and is appropriate for you."

"What do you mean by that?" Anita asks, in exasperation.

I grin. "Actually, I said it very clearly. How do you know that journeying out of your body is something that you need to develop?"

Anita shrugs. "I don't."

"Exactly. Each night when you sleep, you go into five basic cycles of sleep, each lasting about an hour and a half. As you go deeper into a cycle, you move into rapid eye movement (REM) sleep. At this stage of sleep, it is normal for your metaphysical astral body to leave your physical body for a few hours, minutes, or just a few seconds. You generally experience this as powerful, full-colour dreams. This is normal for everyone. Without the astral body leaving the physical body we would have a rapid breakdown in mental health."

"I've heard of this," Todd says. "It's known as an OOBE."

Bill, Marsha and Anita nod vigorously. Only Peter looks baffled.

I nod. "Yes. In my time it was known as astral projection, but now it is more commonly referred to as an out-of-body experience. Which is ridiculous on a certain level because energetically we are much more out of the body than within it. In fact, if people were to have conscious in-body experiences they would be able to more carefully monitor their bodily health. But we don't do this!

"Anyway, astral projection is when you consciously project/send your aware consciousness away with your astral body as your physical body drifts into sleep. In this way we are able to learn and grow in conscious-ness on an entirely different level. With practice you can choose where to astrally journey, and it can be past, present or future, because, as I have said, all time occupies the same moment. When you have an astral ex-perience based in your future, you may retain a deep memory when the accompanying dream is long forgotten. Often we reach that future mo-ment, and bingo . . . deja vu!"

"Oh gosh, I often wondered about experiencing deja vu," Todd says. "Tell me, are metaphysical journeys safe?"

"They are perfectly safe; however, the one thing that you do not want is to go fearfully. Fear needs to be left out of all OOBEs."

"I would imagine so . . . but why exactly?" Todd asks.

I smile at him. "An astral reality is the same as our so-called physical one. By . . . !"

"Why so-called?" Anita interrupts.

I frown at her. "Anita, please don't interrupt. Listen! As I was about to say, by *so-called* I mean that this world is physical for us. Of the multitude of astral worlds – and we are actually one of them – this world that we call physical is not physical for most of the residents of other astral realms. To the residents of mental and emotional astral worlds *we* are not physical as we experience physicality. And if we went to their worlds – metaphysically,

I have visited a few – their worlds are not physical to us. So *physical* is a term that has a certain meaning to us as physical Beings, yet it also has a completely different meaning to us as metaphysical Beings." I pause. "Are you with me?"

Anita looks at me contritely. "Sorry about the interruption, but as far as understanding you goes . . . I am back in upside-down land."

The others also look at me rather blankly.

I chuckle. "I think Anita is fast becoming a human fruit bat! I'm sorry folks, but in a single day or even a week, I cannot fill in the vast empty spaces of human ignorance regarding the greater reality of life. However, if you practice how to leave the physical body with metaphysical awareness, you will find it possible and quite easy. The reason not to do this fearfully is simply because on this astral level you will very *quickly* manifest your fears. What you fear, you will very quickly experience. Of course, having said this, what you fear in our physical normality you will also manifest and experience . . . but on a much *slower* timescale. Everything happens on a metaphysical level sooner/faster than on a physical level simply because we are no longer locked into a linear time reality.

"This gets interesting regarding our physical death!"

Anita puckers her lips. "This is a more ghoulish aspect."

I grin. "If that's a play on words, it's a good one! Mind you, I've never seen a ghoul . . . if they exist, and I have no wish to. Ghosts, yes, and the no-longer-physically-alive disembodied people who have no idea that they have lost their physical body, but . . . no ghouls! Anyway, I have no intention of taking today's discussion into an explanation of physical death and beyond. If you want to know more I suggest you read *Through the Eyes of Love: Journeying with Pan, Book Three*. In there, I have written about such things quite extensively.

"However, before we leave the topic, I would like to remind you that the metaphysical journeying I do is with the physical body awake while journeying, whereas the OOBE type is when the physical body is asleep while travelling. I not only have my body awake, but I am also aware of what is going on around me. I am not in a trance state, just very deeply relaxed and non-attached."

"I find this fascinating," Marsha exclaims.

"I agree, but you came to me to learn about life and living in a 3-D World, to help you in assisting those disadvantaged people with whom you work. They do not need to know about life after death. They need to know about life *before* death . . . along with millions of other people!

... TWENTY-TWO ...

Intelligence, Wisdom and the Intellect

*If or when a person on their spiritual path reaches the stage
of balancing their brain hemispheres, and of opening their
heart to themselves and thus to humanity, then an energetic
link is created between the heart, the whole brain, and the
pineal. Put simply, this, in turn, makes available the wisdom
of the ages, for wisdom is equally personal and universal.*

—Michael J. Roads

I LOOK OVER AT THE PEOPLE. Marsha and Peter seem to have forgotten to
eat. "Before we get onto the next topic, I suggest that you finish eating and
make yourselves a bit more comfortable."

Peter and Marsha quickly finish their meals and the whole group moves
to sit in the more comfortable seats away from the dining table.

I smile at Todd. "Okay, what's next on the agenda?"

Todd grins back at me. "Well, this is not on the agenda, but the more
I listen to you, the more I hear the wisdom in what you say. Maybe the
topic could come from my question, but seriously, what has happened to
the wisdom of the world? As I listen to *your* wisdom, I am realising just

how rare it is. We seldom hear it on the TV, we never hear it from our politicians and just occasionally we hear it from a true world leader. Where did wisdom go?"

I laugh. "You make wisdom sound like a commodity rather than a pure human expression. But, I agree, wisdom seldom falls from modern lips. Nelson Mandela had wisdom and he went through a gruelling process to acquire it. The question that arises is more basic; *what is wisdom?*"

Todd is nodding. "Yes, this is what I was trying to get at."

"As I said to you at the beginning of the day, everything I talk about connects with everything I talk about. Nothing is separate. So to determine what wisdom is will touch upon some aspects I have already discussed. Today, humanity is dominantly using the left-hemisphere of the brain. There are many books written about this, so I will be brief. Left-brain dominance does not suggest that these people do not, or cannot, use the right-brain, they can and do, but they live their day-by-day life from left-brain dominance. This is the realm of the intellect. The intellect is a brilliant tool that is essential for life as a human Being, but it is a *tool,* not a way of life. Unfortunately, left-brain dominance has made the intellect into a way of life and living . . . and it does not work for us. The modern intellect is usually bereft of intelligence, while overflowing with arrogance. This creates a deadly combination, and we see this combination applied in government and politics on a global scale. Left-brain never seems to realise that clever holds hands with stupid.

"If we were to learn to use our *right*-brain hemisphere, using it in equal measure with our left-brain in our daily lives, we would develop into *whole*-brain people. This is the ideal. This is our way forward. In this way we are able to combine intelligence with the intellect. Today, this ability *is* in many people, but it is *not* in the masses, nor unfortunately, is it in the politics and policies of our world leaders. I teach how to balance the brain hemispheres in my Intensives . . . and how to stimulate and develop the pineal gland. With these in progress, we are on the track of wisdom. As I have said, the pineal is situated between the two hemispheres of the brain. In humanity today, medical science tells us that it is shrinking. It is now the size of a grain of rice, instead of the size of a bean. It has the appearance of a tiny, undeveloped pine cone. As the pineal shrinks, so as incarnate Beings, our future will grow ever more grim. But I have no intention of discussing this line of speculation.

"If or when a person on their spiritual path reaches the stage of balancing the brain hemispheres and opening their heart to themselves and thus to humanity, then an energetic link is created between the heart, the whole brain and the pineal. Put simply, this, in turn, makes available the wisdom of the ages – of eternity, in fact, for this is *spiritual* wisdom but it can be meaningfully, practically and beneficially applied in any and all worldly situations – for wisdom is both universal and personal. A person can be wise, contributing much wisdom in their time, but the essence of their wisdom is immortalised in the world of energy and available to all people in all time . . . so long as they have reached that stage of development. In other words, we create the timing to be wise and to share our personal wisdom along with the timeless wisdom of the ages."

Todd is looking puzzled. "But we can read other people's wisdom. It is written in great literature, spoken and written by great philosophers, and in the Bible, and the Koran and such like. It is physically available."

I nod. "Yes, there is much wisdom in words written by wise men and women, but this is not what I was referring to. I was talking about the wisdom that is *energetically* held in the ethers of eternity. Human wisdom has a far higher frequency than our common foolishness. The frequency of foolishness will last for a long time, but it does have a use-by date. The frequency of pure, *spiritual* wisdom is so high and fine that for as long as there is humanity, this wisdom will be available when a person's energy reaches the same higher frequency."

"Geez . . . and this is through the pineal?" Anita says.

I sigh. "No, Anita, I just explained it. The pineal is involved, but it is when a human reaches a holistic state of consciousness, experiencing the Oneness of all life. And this is very different from the sum of its parts!"

Now Anita sighs. "Okay, I'm lost again. Surely Oneness *is* the sum of the parts! How could it be any other way?"

Sitting back in my chair, I stare at the nearby gum trees, watching the dance of their leaves. Why do I do this? Why do I put myself through this human craziness every so often? I smile. Probably because I Love the universal child that is the humanity of this Earth.

Looking at Anita, I roll my eyes. "*Please, listen.* As I said, all energy is One energy. All humanity, all Nature, the earth . . . all *One* energy. So tell me, Anita, where do the parts come from? Explain this to me."

She grins sheepishly, nodding. "Yeah, okay, when you put it like that I can't argue. But, you have to admit that in everyday life everything seems to be separate from everything else. They are the parts."

I nod. "Yes, I do admit that the illusion of separation is overwhelmingly powerful. It overwhelms our connection with the All, it overwhelms our innate intelligence, it overwhelms our spiritual focus, it overwhelms our relationship with a holistic life, and it completely overwhelms most of humanity. Hence we live in a world of illusions."

"Did you say something earlier about our being able to increase our intelligence? I am reaching the leaking stage. As fast as it goes in, some leaks out," Marsha declares, with a laugh. Then she looks serious. "And I don't want to lose any of this. Thank God for the recorder."

"Yes, I did mention it. We have become dominantly a subconscious species, so we subconsciously use our intellect. This obviously has no relationship with intelligence whatsoever! To use our intelligence, we have to be conscious. This suggests that the more conscious you are, the more intelligence you will use. Genius arises with the human frequency as the heart, whole brain and pineal are all energetically interlinked. There is no way to truly measure human intelligence simply because it depends purely on the person's state of consciousness . . . and that can change; it can increase or decrease. So, Marsha, by being more conscious in your daily life you are actively increasing your ability to connect with intelligence. Intelligence is not a set and fixed measure that you receive at birth. For better or worse, intelligence and your consciousness go hand in hand."

Marsha purses her lips. "I'm not sure whether that is good news or seriously bad news."

I smile. "That, Marsha, is entirely up to you."

. . . TWENTY-THREE . . .

On Pain and Suffering

And a woman spoke saying, 'Speak to us of pain.'
And he said: Your pain is the breaking of the shell
that encloses your understanding. Even as the stone
of the fruit must break that its heart may stand in the
sun, so must you know pain.
And could you keep your heart in wonder at the daily
miracles of your life, your pain would not seem less
wondrous than your joy.
—Kahlil Gibran

I SMILE AT THEM. "And this takes us to our next subject. Which choice you make, Marsha, will determine your life. If it really is bad news for you, and you allow your consciousness to become lower through the self-attack of self-criticism, then life will include more pain, more self-sabotage and ever more suffering. They all go together, but we are not obliged to hold their hands.

"When I was a younger man, my life was rather filled with pain and suffering. I seriously injured my lower spine when I was twenty-nine years of age and as a result I suffered for the next twenty years. My spiritual path was one of pain and suffering. Whenever I talk about this, as I reminisce through the years, I marvel at my sheer stupidity. I had no idea that where you focus, your energy flows. If someone greeted me with, 'Hi Michael, how are you?' I would talk to them about my *bad* back. Unbeknown to me, 'bad back' was my focus, and 'bad back' is what I got. Remember what I have constantly told you, we are the creators of our lives and pain and suffering are probably the most common creations of all."

"And they are *very easy* to create," Anita chimes in.

"And pain and suffering is not just physical," Peter adds. "I have had little physical pain in my life, but I have had volumes of mental and emotional pain and suffering."

I smile at him. "Well said. From a metaphysical viewpoint, pain and suffering are a measure of our resistance to change. I remember how I used to invoke change with all my considerable energy and then, in exactly the same measure, I would resist the change that I invoked. I used to think that change would take only the undesirables out of my life. I soon learned that change is like a tornado in your life, ripping and shredding away everything to which you are emotionally attached. And, of course, I resisted. This is almost certainly the main reason we all resist change. We fear it. We truly fear the unknown. We cling to the familiar, even if it is full of pain and suffering. Over many incarnations, we inadvertently create and endure an enormous amount of suffering. I have probably said this before, but suffering is the greatest addiction in humanity. Whether it be through alcohol or drugs, or hate and warfare, or anger and spite, or great wealth or poverty, or through the most common avenues of self-attack, we create our own suffering."

"In our line of work, we encounter self-attack and suffering all the time. Why is it so common? For every person who is self-supportive, there seems to be a hundred into self-attack. Why is this?" Peter asks.

I nod. "Without going back into previous discussions, I have to remind you that self-attack and suffering are very much tied in with subconscious living. The human subconscious is full of the suffering of the past. Living with an attachment to *more of the same* indicates that the reasons and causes for self-suffering endlessly repeat, along with the result . . . more suffering. And so it continues. I am living proof – along with many others – that by being more conscious we are able to grow beyond the grip of suffering.

"Worry creates anxiety, anxiety creates worry; combined together, they are the foundation of many of the plethora of human illnesses. A man once told me that *worry is interest paid on troubles not yet due*. He was not a wise man, he had read it somewhere, but what he said was in perfect timing for me. Worry is *always* based in a mythical future. This means that worry very effectively sabotages the moment, destroying its greater potential. And most people worry. My father was a very clever man; he was also full of anxiety and worry. He seemed to worry about anything and everything. He frowned a lot, developing worry lines in his face, and died in his early sixties. It speaks volumes to me that the clever intellect creates worry, it never comes from intelligence. It is ironic that the warriors of past incarnations are often the worriers of today."

"Are you saying that suffering is deliberately inflicted?" Peter asks.

"Hmm . . . a good question. No, I am not saying that, but *I am saying* that we subconsciously inflict suffering upon ourselves with great deliberation. If a person has no idea that they are creating the content and direction of their life in every moment, then worry and anxiety are considered as part and parcel of everyday life. Worry has become normal because everyone does it. But that worry and anxiety is slowly killing them. It eventually physically manifests as sickness in their body and their bodies suffer before they die.

"Another way of suffering is less obvious. When my late wife entered her transition in 2006, I was bereft with grief. About two weeks after the funeral, I was in the garden with a large, thick, heavy plant pot, attempting to turn it upside-down. Later I realised that it had some potting soil clinging to the inside base. As it thumped over, the soil fell, blasting with the trapped air out of the three drainage holes in the bottom. One of those holes directed a blast of sandy soil straight into my left eye. Within a week I was blind in that eye. As a result of this, about three months later I experienced the miracle of modern surgery in the form of a vitrectomy."

"What's that?" Anita pipes up.

"They went in through the eyeball and with a laser sealed off the capillaries that had bled and/or were bleeding, then cleaned up the debris. The result was that I recovered my eyesight. Later, when I was reflecting on this, I realised that in the very act of grieving, we are inadvertently attacking ourselves. Consciousness does not know the difference between grief and self-attack. How many people would realise that? It is a fact, whether recognised or not, that grief attacks the body; mostly the heart and lungs. So self-contained grief can literally precipitate such an experience as I have mentioned. Of course, modern society would dismiss this as nonsense, calling it just an accident. For consensus reality, accidents happen. For the master, there is no such thing as an accident. For example, being blind in one eye brought up the question; what was I not fully seeing in my life? As I pondered this, I had to accept that Treenie's transition was not by chance, or accident. Having no fear or belief in death, she wanted to go Home – as she called it. I was acting like a victim and I clearly saw how very deep and strong my emotional attachment to her truly was. And as much as I wanted to deny it, an emotional attachment is *not* Love!

"Another incident that happened in the same timeframe enforced this message. It was with my wedding ring. I hung it on a secure gold chain around my neck. One day when I returned from a lonely walk on the beach, I was horrified to find that the unbroken chain was still around my neck . . . but no ring. How was this possible? I drove back to the beach and retraced my footsteps over and over, but to no avail. Very clearly life was saying to me, 'you are no longer married, let go', yet I continued to cling, retaining my emotional attachment to her for another year, until finally, *unconditional* Love prevailed. We all have such experiences or moments, ignoring the signs and messages that life offers us."

"Does this sort of thing happen often with a death?" Anita asks.

I nod. "Probably far more often than is generally realised. But certainly not always. Equally, not every wife or husband is grief stricken by the death of their spouse. Quite often it is a huge relief. My late mother-in-law was married to her husband for over sixty years. At their Diamond Wedding Anniversary, they looked like the perfect devoted couple. What a lie! For the last twenty of those years she had to take angina tablets for her heart. When her husband died, within a few months she stopped taking the angina tablets because she no longer needed them. She lived into her late nineties. He had been, literally, a pain in her heart. He was certainly not a lost love!

"We have a strange relationship with pain. Pain is not exactly as it appears to be. When I was a young man I watched a guy give himself a hypnotic suggestion that his left arm was not *his* arm. He then firmly pushed a long, old fashioned hat pin right through the fleshy part of his arm and into the lightweight coffee table on which his arm rested. Gripping the top of the pin, he lifted his arm and the table into the air. No pain. Sitting right in front of him, I saw it all very clearly. That had a huge effect on me. What happened to the pain? There was no pain because he did not create it. So do we create pain when we are hurt, or is pain inflicted regardless? I suspect that both are true.

"I was once leaning in a doorway talking with friends, unaware that three of my fingers were in the door jamb, where it hinges. My late wife walked through the door and closed it. As she did so I heard a terrible scream. It was me. As she snatched the door back open, my three crushed finger-tips were free. The pain was excruciating. I then made the mistake of putting my fingers under a cold water tap. More agony. This was lunchtime, and in an hour I had to resume my weekend seminar. I asked everybody to leave me alone, which they did. I then lay down, and with my conscious imagination I imagined pink light slowly trickling downward from the crown chakra, through my shoulder and continuing down through my arm, into my hand, and then on into and through my fingers. I imagined the pain being pushed out of my fingers, exiting them as grey/black energy. Within ten minutes I had no pain in my badly crushed fingers, and I was able to continue and finish the seminar."

"Wow . . . that's pretty good," Anita says. "Did they heal okay?"

I nod. "Thank you, yes they did. This incident taught me a lot about focus. When such a thing happens we normally scream with pain and then we focus on the pain and on how bad it is. Inadvertently, we increase it with our fearful focus. I did not do that. I did the opposite and the pain vanished, when, quite honestly, it almost seems that it should not have done so. Once again, we are never-ending creation and we can increase or decrease our own pain. At the risk of constantly repeating it, where we focus, our energy flows. And the energy we focus *with* also determines the outcome."

"You mentioned earlier that you had twenty years of back pain. As I have watched you today and, I confess, with a critical focus, it is clear that you are not in any pain at all. Back pain is serious stuff. How did you get rid of it? Did you have a vertebrae fusion or something like that?" Peter asks.

I chuckle. "Hmm . . . an interesting question. It also brings up the question of our relationship with pain and the consciousness of pain. Such things that are seldom considered. Okay, without going into the whole story which is well-documented in my book which Todd has read, *A Glimpse of Something Greater,* in the very moment of my spiritual enlightenment, my back self-healed. Briefly, one moment I am on the floor in terrible pain, but going through an inner process of surrender, and the next moment I am filled with Love and Light, and for twenty minutes in a different reality. When I came out of this, my body was healed. No back pain or any other of the sicknesses that had been with me."

"That sounds incredible," Peter says. "But what happened?"

"As I said, you can read the full story and all the details. But what actually happened was that I took a leap in conscious of such a magnitude that my body was completely healed. My whole relationship with myself changed in that moment, and with it my relationship with life changed and my relationship with the consciousness of pain."

"I have honestly never heard anything like it," Peter declares.

"Is that what they call a quantum leap?" Anita asks.

I nod. "Yes, a quantum leap in human consciousness."

"This is why you are so . . . er, different?" she asks.

I laugh. "Not so very different, but yes, I guess it is."

... TWENTY-FOUR ...

The Evolution of Consciousness

All life is about the evolution of consciousness. Not just
human life, but all life . . . and this, of course, includes
Nature. We tend to be rather dismissive of Nature,
as though it is something less than us. This
is an error of epic proportions. We are One with Nature.
There is no Nature and humanity; there is no 'and'.
We are One energy expressing in very different ways.
                                                        —Michael J. Roads

BILL CATCHES MY EYE. "In everything you speak about, the word
consciousness repeatedly comes into it. In every explanation you mention
consciousness. I understand why you do this – I think – but please, what
is consciousness?"

I smile at him. "Hmm . . . what indeed? This is the *BIG* question. I could
say that consciousness is the prime mover of life, and that would be true. I
could say that consciousness is entirely passive, with no motivation at all,
and that would be true. The dichotomy of both as One. Does this make
sense?"

"I'm ready to have my world turned upside down, again. But no, to me that does not make sense," Anita responds, with a laugh.

I smile at her. "Let's begin with the basic principle of life concerning consciousness. *Consciousness draws to itself physical form through which to express, but the **expression** is consciousness.* Do you understand that?"

"I'm sure I should, but I am so stuffed with all that you have been telling us that I'm finding it a bit difficult to concentrate," Anita says apologetically.

"Okay, I'll go right to the quintessence of consciousness. In humanity, it is all about being aware of one's existence, or being self-aware. Science does not consider that Nature has consciousness, because according to them, Nature is not self-aware. However, from my metaphysical viewpoint, it is far greater and more complex than this. A tree is not self-aware, true, but a tree is a different expression of consciousness. It seems that science recognises only the human consciousness. Maybe they overlook the fact that we share this planet with a multitude of conscious life forms. In fact, as already stated, we, by living subconsciously, are the least conscious of these life forms.

"Consider a rock, or a mountain. Both of these are expressions of consciousness in which the movement in the moment is i-n-c-r-e-d-i-b-l-y . . . s-l-o-w. In an animal, consciousness is much faster moving, far more dynamic in its expression. In humanity, it is our intellect that is most involved with consciousness, rather than our *whole* Being. Intellect defines and makes a determination on what consciousness is, but the intellect seldom consciously *experiences* it. This leads to false information which eventually becomes false knowledge – and therefore, not *actually* 'knowledge' at all. Crazy! To be fully conscious we are required to be conscious of being conscious in the moment. It becomes obvious that pure consciousness cannot be seen, or captured, or bottled, although we can capture and retain those creatures which *express* consciousness.

"Consciousness is universal. In our galaxy there are conscious life forms that are far beyond our own consciousness and others that are way behind our potential expression. I say potential simply because we all express our personal consciousness in different ways; some generously, some grudgingly, some aggressively, some peacefully, and so on. Whereas if you consider rabbits, for example, all rabbits express consciousness in very much the same way. Humanity is individualising consciousness, as are some of the higher animals, whereas for flocks and herds of animals and birds it is more a herd or flock consciousness.

"To summarise this, consciousness is the energy that permeates, animates, and energises all natural life-forms in the mineral, vegetable and animal kingdoms . . . including us. Sure, we use consciousness individually and uniquely, but certainly not exclusively."

Peter stares at me intently. "What so impresses me – and challenged me – is that you embody the energy of your words, of your knowledge, your *knowing*. I have attended hundreds of lectures and I connected to a degree, but the knowledge always remained in my head. With you, the inner *knowings* that you describe have entered into me, somehow reaching into places that I did not know was possible. This is so different. It alarmed me at first and I strongly resisted, but something in me broke down, like some old barrier, and as it broke I felt a new freedom. How can I thank you for something like that?"

I smile at him. "Very easily . . . by living it. That's all the thanks I need."

Bill laughs. "Okay, you have definitely answered my question about consciousness. I intend to listen to my copy of the recording many times. I also need to say how today has enriched my life. I'll never be the same again. I only hope Mary can embrace the new me . . . although personally, I think she will be delighted. Thank you so very much."

"We have a few hours yet, so I'll continue with consciousness, but with a word of caution. Of all the many topics I have discussed with you, please do not jump to conclusions. I do not recommend that you draw conclusions."

"Er . . . what is wrong with conclusions?" Anita asks.

I smile. "I recommend that you avoid conclusions. A conclusion is the closing of a door, the mind, on a certain aspect in our lives. Suppose the conclusion is completely wrong? Best to avoid closing the door and simply move on in life with the door ajar. In right timing, a life-changing *knowing* can come through that is not possible with a closed door."

"Is this the same as closure?" Anita persists.

I nod at her. "A very good point. No; conclusions are mental, intellectual, while closure is about our emotions, our feelings. Closure is fine, but it pertains to the normal, short-term view of life. When you *know* there is no death, closure is not necessary. I am perfectly content in knowing that my late wife is living her life to the full . . . without me. I accept that. When you acquire emotional balance, closure is not something that you need or look for. However, closure offers huge emotional comfort when life is lived with the normal belief in beginnings and endings. Closure is an ending, even if it is not real. In all probability the storyline will continue in the next incarnation.

"They were a couple of good questions, Anita. However, may I now move on with our discussion on consciousness?"

She smiles cheekily. "You have my permission."

I chuckle. "Thank you. All life is about the evolution of consciousness. Not just human life, but *all* life . . . and this, of course includes Nature. We tend to be rather dismissive of Nature, as though it is something less than us. This is an error of epic proportions. We are *One* with Nature. There is no Nature *and* humanity, there is no *and*. We are One energy expressing in very different ways. Do you remember what I said at the beginning of this, after Bill asked me what is consciousness?"

They all look at me guiltily, slightly caught out by the question.

"I'll repeat it. *Consciousness draws to itself physical form through which to express, but the **expression** is consciousness.* When you fully understand this on a heart level, feeling it, you will have a deeper connection with Truth. Unfortunately, it usually remains only as an intellectually understood mental statement, with no real connection to the Truth of the principle."

I smile at them. "Hopefully, you can do better. All life is about the evolution of consciousness. It is not the physical form that evolves, even though that goes through improvements in accord with the evolving state of consciousness. We are very much physical-form oriented, believing ourselves to be bodies. If some people are killed in a multiple-car collision, the TV newsfeed will announce how many lives were lost. In Truth, no lives are ever lost. Physical form is lost, but that was never *the life* of a person. Life and consciousness are one and the same. We have great confusion in these areas. We talk about the great *collective unconscious*, but there is no such thing. Consciousness can never be un-conscious, or not-conscious, any more than consciousness can be un-life. If you hit me on the head with a lump of wood and I fall to the floor, you would describe me as unconscious. In Truth, you have immobilised my brain, interrupting my brain's connection with consciousness. This, in turn, means that with my brain switched off, my body is immobilised. When we have an operation and we are anaesthetised, we are so-called *unconscious*. This actually means that we are no longer *conscious* of being conscious! Stay with me! Several people have repeated verbatim much of the conversation that took place around their anaesthetised body while they were being operated on. This has been well-documented. What I am saying is that our language, combined with the illusion in which people live, has created our false beliefs and misconceptions of what consciousness truly is."

"Are you saying that Freud and Jung are wrong?" Marsha asks.

"I'm saying that within their limitations they have made statements that are not part of a greater holistic reality. Their teachings were appropriate for the times, but, quite frankly, they no longer are appropriate. When we continually refer to the past for understanding, then we will walk backward to the future, rather than forward. In other words, as is proven, history repeats itself. We are that history. We are the past, the present and the future all occupying the same moment in eternity."

"Oh God . . . you're doing it again. I'm upside down and hopelessly lost," Anita says. "How can we be in the past, in the now and the future all simultaneously, or did I misunderstand you?"

"No, you did not misunderstand me. When you relate to life on a holistic level, you see and experience it differently. As you well know, many movies and books have the theme of time travel, following many of the incarnations of their heroes and villains as they intercept each other's lives in, mostly, endless conflict. The movie ends and pizza is served and the movie is now forgotten. Seldom do people ask themselves, if life is now, how can there be life in the past simultaneously? They accept the book or movie at face value only. Well, all life and the experience of it is simultaneous. What this basically means is that all the people who have ever lived are still living in their own timeline frame of reality. Science is seriously investigating time travel. Do you think they would do this if the past was empty of life? Of course not. This whole timeline area can get very confusing, so much so that most people dismiss it. But think, if a person dies, losing their body, are they still alive in the previous years of their life, which is the past?"

"And the answer is?" asks Todd.

"Because death is an imposter, and because we are not actually physical people locked in a physical timeframe, the answer is yes, they are still alive in all the *total* timeline of their previous lives *and* their not yet realised or experienced future."

"Okay . . . enough," Anita says. "I'll go potty with more of this."

I chuckle. "Holistic life is not just a word or description. Holistic life means that we live all life simultaneously and timelessly. This is part and parcel of our evolution of consciousness. And it is not just us. Consider, if you will, the estimated two hundred *million* years that the dinosaurs lived here. The boffins estimate that we have been here about two hundred *thousand* years. In fact, we are at the closing of the fifth, two hundred thousand year cycle. We have been here far longer than supposed. But when you consider the dinosaurs' time on Earth, you must be aware that this also was/is about the evolution of consciousness. I mean, after two hundred *million* years of evolution, do you honestly believe that the various species of dinosaurs were the stupid, dumb creatures we suppose them to be? And they have had a huge period of time to continue with their conscious evolution since their known time on Earth! Life is far, far more vast than we realise. Life is not a single stream of consciousness moving toward some great central lake; life is countless, endless streams of consciousness moving toward an eventual convergence of consciousness on such a colossal scale that it will cause a quantum explosion of potential in all appropriate lifeforms. It would not surprise me in the least if many of the dinosaur species are now far beyond our own human level of consciousness. We are capable of great cruelty, of terrible crimes, of wholesale slaughter and of the ability to inflict horrific torture on our fellow Beings. Yet, we are also capable of great and compassionate acts of Love and kindness. But at some future point, when we meet the dinosaur Beings, we may well find that we are the primitives, and they the civilised!"

"I'll never be able to watch Jurassic Park and such like and enjoy them again," Anita laments.

I laugh. "We seldom realise our lives are as make-believe as a movie. It's all a great game of make-believe. And then, when the physical body reaches its use-by date, we continue the same stupid game on a purely metaphysical level of reality. Of course, if you are more conscious and aware, actually *evolving* in consciousness, then the after-physical-death experience is very different. We meet our soul guides, learn the principles of Truth all over again, have a time of rest, relaxation and reflection, and meet with our real soul families. And all this in a period of timelessness. With our soul guide we create a game-plan for our next incarnation, while attempting to put off that awful moment for as long as we can! We probably consider each incarnation as the death of freedom! Forget death . . . it would be more accurate to say that we are born from the metaphysical into the physical, and eventually we are born out of the physical back into the metaphysical."

"Is it like this for everybody?" Marsha asks.

I smile at her. "Back to the earlier principle. *In every moment of your life you are creating the content and the direction of every moment of your life.* In every moment' means just that. Not while you are physical only, but every moment of your forever-life and living. If you are creating hell for yourself in your physical life, you will continue in the metaphysical . . . much to your great shock and consternation."

Todd sighs deeply. "I suppose that spiritual enlightenment is a great leap in consciousness. Considering your words about Oneness, does a single person's enlightenment affect everyone?"

"I think I mentioned this, but yes, not that anyone will notice. Just as great acts of kindness and terrible acts of cruelty touch us all on a deeper level of consciousness, so one person's spiritual enlightenment has a soul connection with all souls. One energy! It is the souls we are that grow in consciousness. Unlike a body builder who will one day lose it, the growth and development of a soul is forever."

I look at my five guests as they regard me. "I can see and feel that you are all a bit tired, but I am more energised than when we began. Why is this? Simply put, I have been skating over the universal pond of Truth, feeling *empowered* by it, while you have all been testing the ice to see if it will bear your weight. Trust me . . . it will. If I speak or write words of communication that carry any deliberate, or ego-based, falsehood and a single person is damaged by what I have communicated, then I am also damaged by this. I lose energy. I lose lustre. I lose my connection with Truth. Trust me . . . this does not happen. In my world, I am you and you are me, in *Oneness*. To me, the relationship between us is a sacred trust;

I Love you."

With these last three words, the men all look hugely embarrassed.

Not so Anita. She comes to me and envelops me in a fierce hug.

"And I Love you," she whispers, loudly and dramatically. "You are amazing. I don't know how to thank you enough, but I will be at your next Intensive. That's for sure."

. . . TWENTY-FIVE . . .

Good and Evil – Right and Wrong

The illusion says that there are accidents, and that inadvertently, evil happens. Truth offers a different picture. Truth says that we are immortal Beings, and that if we do someone serious evil, then we will be stuck with that action as, over lifetimes, we experience the reactions and repercussion of what we did. We are stuck with evil until we have learned the lesson of our own creation.

—Michael J. Roads

PETER SHAKES HIS HEAD GENTLY. "Well, you certainly answered Bill's question. I don't fully get it, but I fully get why I don't fully get it!"

Everyone laughs, along with Peter.

I look pensively at the group. "Okay, what's your next topic?"

Todd looks as though he is emerging from a dream. "The complexities of consciousness, whew! Okay . . . one of the topics we have on our list is good and bad, right and wrong, that sort of thing."

I nod thoughtfully. "Yes, that makes sense in your line of work. Most people definitely believe in evil. This becomes very apparent in all our movies with the themes of goodies and baddies, and the malevolent evil in so many horror movies." I smile. "Not that I ever see them. I'm very careful and discerning with what I put into my energy-field. We . . . "

"Sorry to interrupt, but what does that mean, exactly?" Anita asks.

I nod at her. "Fair enough. Back to my old and regular adage; where you focus your energy flows . . . and *creates*. Imagine, as you watch a horror movie, the emotions that the movie is creating in you. In a way they are voluntary emotions because you unwisely chose to see the movie, and in another way the emotions are involuntary because the perceived horror is creating them. The end result is emotional confusion, accompanied by a seriously flawed energy – horror. This gets interesting: consciousness knows nothing of movies and play-horror; consciousness knows only what is happening to your emotions. This horror is now part of your life story. Your left-brain says, 'Don't be silly, it's just a movie', but the intellect knows nothing of life. You are energy/consciousness and you have just introduced horror into the state of consciousness that is you. Do you honestly think that life is going to be happier after this, or more *uplifting*? If you are a regular viewer of horror movies – and millions are – then horror will eventually enter your life in whatever way is appropriate to you."

Anita stares at me, appalled. "Are you serious?"

I smile. "I certainly am. Every life is self-created. You can accept that, or dismiss it. If you accept it you will find that the people who go through horrific trauma in their life have been involved with horror. Nothing is by accident, nothing by chance. If you reject it, then you go with the common illusionary belief that accidents happen. Your choice!"

"Why is it that the more I learn from you, the scarier life gets?" Anita asks, with a look of exaggerated horror.

"Actually, it doesn't," I reply. "The more you learn from me, the more you realise how many unwise choices you have made that did not serve you. Some definitely harmed you. Choosing me was one of your wiser choices!"

She laughs. "Okay . . . I have to agree."

"Good and evil, along with right and wrong, are not real outside of the illusion. They accompany our *perceptions* of life. They are concepts created by the society we live in. Sure, I agree, we all have a common accord about the good things in life, and maybe about the good deeds in life, but we have different feelings about what is or isn't evil. There is a common saying; while good men do nothing, evil flourishes. This is very understandable, but it belongs in the illusions of life. The illusion says that there are accidents and that inadvertently, evil happens. Truth offers a different picture. Truth says that we are immortal Beings and that if we do someone serious evil, then we will be stuck with that action as, over lifetimes, we experience the reactions and repercussion of what we did. We are stuck with evil until we have learned the lesson of our own creation.

"When a person comes along – like Idi Amin, for example, a man who was considered responsible for about a million deaths – then everyone on a soul level who, from their own earlier creations, needs to be on the receiving end of evil and horror, incarnates within the influence of that man. In this way they have an intimate experience of what they once, long ago in another lifetime/incarnation, themselves created. The pity is, rather than grow from such a chance to balance their energy, they get lost in the illusionary world of blame, anger and the assumption of evil. Equally, all that Idi Amin sows, he too, will reap! And so it continues, on and on. This is a view of a greater reality; the Truth of evil. Right and wrong is more subtle, not so easy to define."

"Very thought provoking," Marsha says. "But I'll bet *you* can define right and wrong, even if it isn't easy."

"I'll do my best. Right and wrong are no more than two ends of an argument. But, each person involved thinks that they are right and the other is wrong. So who is right? Quite often neither of them is, simply because right and wrong are not applicable . . . they have differing opinions! It has been said that nothing is right or wrong, thinking makes it so. Very true.

"Consider this: a couple of hundred years ago, in Australia, an aboriginal man is walking along on a beach. He is a hunter, so he is vigilant of all Nature around him. Suddenly he sees a large turtle in the waves near the shore and, plunging into the water, he grabs the turtle and with great effort drags it high up onto the beach. Then, with more exertion, he turns the turtle over onto its back. He then walks away, leaving the poor animal in a helpless position, unable to turn itself right-side up. He keeps on walking, unconcerned for it, eventually disappearing into the salt haze further along the beach. Today, we would consider this as a purposefully cruel action, and that he was very wrong to do this. He, on the other hand, is a hunter. His family is a couple of days or so behind him on the shoreline and, when they reach the turtle, food will be waiting for them. He does not have the luxury of a beachfront home with electricity and a modern refrigerator where he could put the quickly-killed and butchered meat. He has to make do with what he has and feed his family. Is he wrong?"

Marsha sighs, shaking her head. "You make a very good point. How can he be wrong if you look at it from his viewpoint?"

"I have heard that the well-known, enlightened master, Krishnamurti, used to tell a little story that goes something like this. I may have the details a bit skewed, but the essentials are there. He was with three European men on a slow journey through some of the more remote villages in India. Their progress in an old vehicle came to a stop when they encountered a man and his huge bull, making their slow way along the centre of the dusty and narrow road. The man's living was made by taking the bull from village to village, there to service the few cows that most families owned. For a while the vehicle, along with Krishnamurti and his small group, was forced to just follow the man and his bull. They noticed that every so often the man would lift a slender cane and hit the bull across his testicles to keep him moving. The men complained to Krishnamurti, telling him that he should stop the man inflicting such blatantly unnecessary pain on the bull. It was very wrong.

Krishnamurti smiled at them indifferently. 'Why should I do this? The men who own the bulls have been doing it this way for centuries. It is what they do. Do you think for a moment they are going to damage the bull's testicles, when their very livelihood depends on their perfect function? They long ago learned that such a massive animal will only respond if lightly flicked on their most sensitive part, rather than violently beaten on their hides."

I chuckle. "Right and wrong go hand-in-hand with bigotry and bias. I have no doubt that the prejudiced people in the Ku Klux Klan think that they are right, but people with no racial hatred say they are wrong. Opinions! But, as I have said, *we do have and need* a common agreement of right and wrong. We very much need this in a society that lives fearfully in illusion. We need to create behavioural boundaries for people who are

140

unable to set them for themselves. I find it fascinating that some of the more extreme religions, that preach hellfire and damnation, are far more into screaming about the evil in people than they are about the good in people. What attracts people to such a religion? I can only assume it is their own inherent self-hatred. When they can scream hate about other people, it probably relives their own self-hate for a little while."

"We see such themes in movies," Marsha says.

"Yes, we do. I enjoy a good movie, but I do not *need* a movie. For many and varied reasons it would appear that many people need their movies. Maybe it is boredom with themselves. I have seen the Rambo movies on the TV screen. Very interesting. Those movies inadvertently promote the idea, or concept, that vengeance is good, right, and justified. And they also promote the idea that the more evil the perpetrators of evil are, then the more violent the vengeance should be that is visited upon them. Such a theme certainly created a lot of money for Sylvester Stallone. And that's okay. But it is our world of movies and books that keep the concept of good and evil and right and wrong alive and kicking in the everyday lives of ordinary people."

"And I'm right in there with the best of them, wanting the goodies to kick the butts of the baddies," Anita says, with a laugh.

"Don't we all?" Bill adds.

I nod. "Me, too. If I'm going to deliberately play with illusion I might as well enjoy it! But I have to say that I far prefer the feel-good movies."

"I can see what you were saying," Peter says, "particularly in the Idi Amin example, but does this imply that in the Second World War all the people involved in the battles, whichever side they were on, incarnated to be part of that experience? I find such a concept breathtaking."

"Yes, that is exactly what I am implying. Remember . . . nothing by accident, nothing by chance. And not only the people in the armies, or actively involved in the battles, but also the people in the bombed cities, devastated families, everyone affected by the warfare, all the so-called victims. It is all part of an endless soul movie aiming toward people finding balance."

"Balance! What does balance have to do with it?" Bill puts in.

... TWENTY-SIX ...

Universal Balance

*Harmony is the result of perfect balance. If an orchestra
is in harmony, then the music will be in perfect balance.
Can you imagine the quality of the music if everyone in
the orchestra had perfect balance in their own personal
lives? Such music has never been heard by physical
human ears . . . but it exists.*

—Michael J. Roads

I LOOK AT BILL IN SURPRISE. "Balance has everything to do with it. In
fact, balance has just about everything to do with just about everything!"

"Meaning what . . . exactly?" Bill asks. "Please explain."

"Okay, universal balance is a good subject. The people you counsel, do
they have balance in their lives? No, they don't, in fact they are far from it.
But consider this, if they had balance in their lives, would they then come
to you for help? Would they need it?"

Bill nods in agreement. "Probably not. I see your point."

"Okay, be patient with me on this," I ask. "In our constellation in space
we have black holes. Not much is known about them, although there is
plenty of constantly changing speculation. Obviously, my view of black

142

holes would be considered laughable. Nevertheless, from my metaphysical perspective, a black hole is a region within space-time exhibiting such strong gravitational effects that nothing – not even the electromagnetic energy of light – can escape from inside it. Yet it is not trapped. From my perspective, a black hole is a form of incredible universal balance."

I smile all round at their surprised and slightly sceptical expressions.

"Okay, let's look at this. Seen from a 3-D perspective, space is vast beyond measure. Seen from a metaphysical perspective, it is not quite as it appears in 3-D. To me, space is a vast holographic, yet very real, cosmic energy depiction of epic holistic proportions. In 3-D we have time and distance, but metaphysically they are not part of the space equation. Within this spacious vastness, everything is energy in zillions of different expressions and countless dimensions. It is all holistic, but physically, we see it only as 3-D. This is similar to taking the contents out of a kaleidoscope and laying them out flat. We no longer get the same kaleidoscopic effect. Yet this is the way we physically see space and believe it to be. We do not see the true holistic picture.

"Throughout the universe energy is in dynamic action and yet, like a flowing river, there are always some backwaters where the energy is slowed to the point of becoming stagnant. Just as this will have an adverse influence on the whole river system, so, too, on a far greater scale, it has an overall detrimental effect on the flow of universal energy, simply because all energy is One."

I look at the group. "Are you still with me?"

I receive a series of cautious nods.

"This is where the balancing act comes in. When energy is stuck, inert, stagnant, on such a vast universal scale that our own Milky Way Galaxy would appear as a scattering of grains of sand, the repercussions are far-reaching. This is where the black holes come in. They irresistibly attract and pull into themselves vast areas of stagnant space and everything within it. In this process, creation is compelled from inert stagnation to becoming active and vibrant." I pause, thinking. "It's difficult for me to find the words. Okay, this physical and metaphysical alchemy of universal proportions creates a total energetic transformation of both physical and metaphysical matter as it is continually expelled from the black hole into a completely different section of universal space. And it is not expelled randomly, as we might expect. There is *order* behind the apparently chaotic actions of black holes that is far beyond human definition. Let's simply say that Supreme Creation leaves nothing to chance, for chance is a human concept.

"However, my point is that if something of the magnitude of a universe needs to be continually balancing for the wellbeing of all forms of life, then we certainly need to pay homage to balance regarding our life on Earth."

"But we are told that everything that is sucked into a black hole is annihilated," Peter protests. "How can this be for the wellbeing of all life?"

I nod. "Point taken. But you are overlooking the fact that all life is metaphysical energy, not physical form. So, immortality always persists. Metaphysically I have been into a black hole. *(Stepping Between Realities)* Trust me, it was nothing like I expected. Science has given birth to the belief that black holes are death to life. I experienced it in reverse. I consider that black holes give life to death."

Anita looks at me with raised eyebrows. "Are you for real? I mean, how is it possible to enter a black hole and live? And yet, crazy I may be, but I believe you. You are probably the most sane person I have ever met."

I give her a big, wide smile. "Thank you. I probably am! So . . . if the universe is prepared to expend so much energy to create endless universal balance, then we would be wise to ensure that we have balance in our *personal* lives. Anger is an out-of-balance expression, along with so many of our negative emotions."

"Out of balance with what?" Bill asks.

"Out of balance with harmony. As I have said, and probably will again, disease *is* out of harmony with health. Dis-ease literally means lack of ease: discord rather than harmony. Harmony is what results from perfect balance. If an orchestral concert is in perfect harmony, then the sound of music is in balance. But can you imagine the quality of the music if everyone in the orchestra had perfect balance in their own personal lives? Such music has never been heard by physical human ears . . . but it exists. If I was asked to create a name for God that actually defines God's reality, it would be, The Endless Song of Infinite Balance."

"Oh . . . I like that," Anita breathed. "The word God conveys nothing to me other than an unfathomable concept, but *The Endless Song of Infinite*

Balance creates images that I can relate to, and embrace."

"That description is not my creation, I borrowed it," I tell her. "Many years ago I read a booklet about an enlightened life, and God was described in such a manner. It touched me very deeply.

"I consider that Nature offers the most perfect examples of the endless ebb and flow of balance," I continue. "Sun and rain balance, night and day balance, hot and cold balance. Sure, some areas are continuously cold and some continuously hot, but globally these are in balance. Droughts balance floods, even though they both cause havoc in their areas of influence. The planet is invested in global balance, rather than local balance. Today, imbalance is wreaking havoc within Nature, but the imbalances come from humanity. We are a very imbalanced species."

"But doesn't Nature create imbalance?" Bill asks. "Consider the vast herds of bison that used to roam the prairies of America. A million mouths grazing the land simultaneously would have to cause massive imbalance."

I smile at him. "Actually, no. The million mouths grazed the grassland, and a million bums expelled fertiliser for the grassland . . . and the bison moved on. They did not return until the following season, when they were greeted by lush, naturally-fertilised native grasses all perfectly in balance with the graze-and-fertilise cycle that was created by Nature. But, as we know, within a few years the invading white hunters from the early migrants broke the bison balance that the Native American Indians had nurtured and maintained for many centuries."

"How would you define perfect balance in a person?" Marsha asks.

"Hmm . . . good question. For me, there is metaphysical balance and physical balance. As I watch the professional surfers on TV, I am always very impressed by their incredible sense of physical balance. When I watch an Olympic diver preparing to dive, there comes a moment when, prior to the dive, they are completely still; this is the place of dynamic stillness. That moment for me represents perfect physical balance in a person. Still, poised, every muscle tense, all in a single accord of balance.

"Then there is metaphysical balance. This is rarely seen in people. I consider that I am in fairly good balance. Not perfect, but getting there. Of course, metaphysical balance is a constant, not something that we attain for a few moments. This is why it is so rare. But, as with the orchestra, if a diver was able to be in metaphysical balance, then physical balance would be easier for their highly-trained bodies to acquire. And each dive would be superlative, a never-yet-seen experience. It would be possible to enter the water in such balance and accord, that scarcely a ripple would be seen. However, when a diver enters the water, the water also needs to be in balance, and that never happens in a swimming pool. The water is dead. If the diver was metaphysically balanced and diving into balanced living water, then wow! that would be something special indeed.

"Balance is a wise personal quest for everyone. If wealth was measured by a person's balance, rather than the balance of a bank account, then we would qualify for the term Homo sapiens. The way we live in the illusion, we are more qualified to be termed Homo Un-sapiens!"

Peter laughs. "Unwise man describes me for most of my life, but I am planning on changing that. I feel as though a large, heavy weight has been lifted off my shoulders, and this is *before* I make the required changes."

I smile at him. "Actually, Peter, just by moving from fixed and stuck to open and flexible is a huge change. And you have already done this. Once you open yourself to life as you have done, then balance is flowing in. You are a perfect example of moving from imbalance to balance. And this is only the beginning. As you become more conscious and aware of your words and actions, of your thoughts and emotions and feelings, so you will continue to move toward ever greater balance.

"I will mention something that I have written about in my trilogy, *Through the Eyes of Love: Journeying with Pan,* so I won't go into detail now. You can read about it if you are interested. When a human and/or an aspect of Nature are in perfect balance, then metaphysically a white light flickers around the physical body of that person, or animal, or tree. It looks a little like Saint Elmo's Fire, which is blue, while the metaphysical light of balance is a pure, flickering, scintillating white. I have never seen it physically, but metaphysically it is quite mesmerising, beautiful."

"Okay, without going into detail, does fear or anger have a metaphysical colour?" Anita asks coyly.

I smile at her. "How can I answer that without detail? Hmm, I'll just give you the bare outline. Everything with life is energy and all energy has an accompanying energy-field of colour. There are three basic energy-fields,

146

each with a huge range of their own colour. For me, I see Chaos as red, with maybe a thousand shades of red. I see Order as black, with about a thousand shades of black . . . and then there is Balance, the brilliant, flickering white. With the words Chaos, Order and Balance, I capitalise them when I write them to indicate that they are not of the same meaning as the world's interpretation of those words. In the Western World we have no words or language for a metaphysical reality, or at least, I don't. I'm aware that Sufism has an esoteric language that gives names to many mystical phenomenon, but not being part of that tradition, the words are meaningless to me."

"Oh . . . come on," says Anita. "That's all very fascinating, but you can't just leave it like that. Give me just a tiny little bit more detail, please." She bats her eyelids at me.

I sigh. "Okay, just briefly, the Chaos to which I refer is not your normal everyday traffic chaos! All that I am describing is metaphysical energy. *Chaos is the engine that drives.* It is essential. A wildfire is Chaos with almost no Order. *Order is the stability of structure.* A stone is Order with almost no Chaos. *Balance is where the torsion between Chaos and Order is equal.* This creates the white light effect. Okay?"

Anita gives me a level stare. "No, not okay. If I promise that I'll read your trilogy, will you give me, us, a bit more detail? I, for one, find this truly and utterly fascinating. And what do you mean by torsion? Please; pretty please!"

I laugh. Anita certainly has the winning way of youth.

"Okay, okay. If you imagine a wet towel, with Todd holding one end and twisting it to the right, and Bill on the other end twisting it to the left, the towel will gradually tighten between them, squeezing out the water. This tightening effect is torsion. If they had the strength to keep on twisting, the towel would eventually break down and disintegrate in the middle from too much torsion. You get that?"

Anita and the others nod.

"Every cell in your body has that torsion built into it as the energies of Chaos and Order interplay in your daily life and living. Chaos and Order do not oppose each other; they create a dynamic that holds the potential for perfect Balance. Fear takes you heavily into Chaos, so as your body cells move away from Balance, they become less flexible. All human dis-eases indicate that Chaos and Order are out-of-harmony."

"But how do you know all this? I mean, who has ever heard anything like this? Or, at least, I never have, and I have never, ever heard of such a thing mentioned by anyone. It sounds very strange," Anita says.

I nod sympathetically. "I'm sure it does. But you don't have to believe me. If the medical profession or other people know nothing of this, then I must surely be wrong. So, dismiss it."

Anita gives me a very vexed glare. "No, I won't. I already know you too well for that. I already have too much respect for your insights and wisdom to dismiss it. So please, please explain how you know all this?"

"I know because we do, in fact, have a *hidden* metaphysical language. It is a language that speaks energetically to the emotions, not the intellect. One day in the distant future, when we are 6-D Beings, we will no longer verbally communicate. We will use a blend of aware emotions along with conscious thoughts blended into an advanced form of telepathy.

"You need to be aware that Chaos is not bad, with Order as good. There is no duality involved, so no human terms for such are applicable. All the hundreds of shades of red Chaos denote different energies of Chaos, like the many types and expressions of anger, the many expressions of fear, of rage, of self-loathing but also of self-acceptance and self-worth, etc. And it's the same with Order. The energy colours communicate, or interact with my emotional body, both creating and releasing an enormous range of deep inner emotions that I recognise, and which translate within me, but for which I have no names, no words. This incredible emotional language transcends words. Metaphysically, I see the different shades of colour in forests and in single trees, according to their health, energy and wellbeing. I see it in crowds and in single people. It is in every cell of every person and in their body as a whole.

"But ... humanity is not yet ready for this. While we live subconsciously, such communication is not possible. We have not yet evolved to the required level of consciousness to accept such a language. We do not have the required balance in our lives. I'm an oddity. I'm the opposite of a dinosaur. A dinosaur is past its timing, in this aspect; I'm ahead of mine."

... TWENTY-SEVEN ...

A Question of Health

As you do your counselling work, you are focusing and creating and connecting. You get that? In every moment, you are creating and connecting. However, you do get to decide what you focus on. If you focus on your client's problem, you connect with it and with their problematic emotional energy. Whereas, if you focus on the solution, you get to connect with this, and with the uplifting energy that it offers.

—Michael J Roads

ANITA STARES AT ME. "Doesn't this make you feel very . . . lonely?"

I look away. "Now you're getting morbid. But yes, to be honest there are moments when I feel achingly lonely, but they are few, and I have Carolyn. She doesn't share my experiences, but she is fully and truly in the spaces of my heart, sharing my energy-field of Love. This is enough. I knew when I moved deeper into the metaphysical world that there would be a price, but I didn't know what it would be. The price is little enough and I pay it happily for the immensity and richness and fullness of the holistic life that I encounter and experience – and, I confess, for the priceless opportunities

149

it provides me to share with those of my beloved humanity who are ready to listen and grow.

"And having spoken about the human energy-field, this indirectly brings us to another topic . . . a question of health"

"So what is the question?" Anita asks cheekily.

I smile at her. She is living proof that youth can get away with a type of cheekiness that in an older person would be considered rather rude.

"The question: why is the great percentage of humanity so sick? We have the *obvious* reasons, such as poor nutrition caused by junk food and junk drink and toxic inhalation through cigarettes, but we have to realise that nobody is compelled to eat or drink or inhale such rubbish. Why do people *do* this? This question brings us once again to our relationship with ourselves. If we have an honouring relationship with ourselves, we do not ingest or imbibe or inhale substances that create a slow death."

"Slow death!" That's a bit strong, isn't it?" Marsha says.

I shake my head. "Not at all. I am convinced that the average person – whoever that is – has very little knowledge about the workings of their body, and takes almost no responsibility for it. This is unwise. They depend on the medical system and the doctors to do this for them. The difficulty with this is that the doctors suffer from many of the same health problems as their patients. If they cannot prevent or cure the health issues in themselves, how can they do this for their patients?

"Among the many useless statistics that are published, one of them is about the life expectancy of people in certain jobs. Apparently, in the group of the longest-lived people are orchestral conductors. I find this fascinating, because from my metaphysical viewpoint, the reason is obvious. To conduct an orchestra you are required to be *fully conscious* in the moment. This is not common. You are required to be within the moment to the extent that you are aware of every note of music from every player in the orchestra. You are deeply involved in *listening*. Listening takes you into the moment, thinking takes you out of it . . . remember? As an orchestral conductor, being in the moment reveals another factor to metaphysical insight. A person connected to the vitality of the moment has a different relationship with linear time than a person who never makes that connection. In a normal state of consciousness we collectively age at a certain speed, although some people progress slower than others and some progress faster. But the more time that is spent consciously engaged in the timeless moment, the less that person is affected by the ageing factor of linear time. It would appear that orchestral conductors are the living proof of this. You will also find that many dedicated artists are in this group, for while deeply immersed in the creativity of a painting, they too are consciously engaging the moment. I would imagine that the same applies to sculptors, and others who spend much of their life in purely creative endeavours."

"So what profession is at the bottom of this statistic?" Marsha asks.

I chuckle. "Interestingly, doctors and dentists and people in the health profession. Apparently it is a hazardous career!"

Marsha looks at me indignantly. "That hardly makes sense."

I smile. "Not to you, maybe, but it does to me. Let's go back to our old adage; where you focus, your energy flows, and creates. We all know that when you go into a busy waiting room at the doctors, it is a low energy. Not a bad energy, but a low one, based in suffering overlaid with fear. The more focused a doctor is on their patients, the more powerfully they energetically connect. We all know that some doctors do not truly connect at all, they simply push prescriptions. But most doctors care about their patients, so they connect. This means that for five days a week their energy is being dragged downward by their energetic connection to their low-energy patients. They work in an energy-field of pain, anger, blame and suffering. As do most of the paramedics, nurses and many hospital workers. It seems almost unfair, but we live in a society that knows nothing of energetic connections and their cost in human suffering.

It is a similar story with the dentist. Many people still dread going to the dentist, although dental treatment today is a hundred times better than when I was a boy. Nevertheless, it is still common for people to fear making a dental appointment. They usually do so under the stimulus of pain. All unrealised, this repetitive energetic connection of fear is often detrimental to the health of the dentist. Although, I repeat, this is getting less so with the advances in gentle dental care. So, all in all, many people who work in health care do not energetically thrive. This often equates to a life shortened by energetic stresses of which almost no one seems to be aware."

Todd is nodding. "Yes, I've encountered these types of statistics. You can include women who work in women's hairdressers in the lower bracket. Chemicals in the hair products are considered the main reason. They work in the chemical fumes all day. Plus many ladies unload their problems on the hairdresser as they chatter. But the question that arises for me . . . is about *us*! We work with other people's problems. People who are hurting, and often angry and demanding. We get very emotionally connected with their energy, so is this going to have a negative effect on our health? And if it is, what can we do about it?"

I nod. "Hmm, yes . . . you're right. You do work with other people's fears and hurts and anger and blame . . . the whole negative caboodle! So, what can you do about it? Indeed, that *is* the question. Another question of health. You three guys are aged about what? Well into your forties? So, how is your current health? I would hazard a guess that it gets slightly worse each year. A downhill trend."

Todd sighs deeply. "Speaking for myself, yes. Each year I take a bit more sickness time off than the year before. Not much, but the trend is there. I figured this was because of my age. Now, looking at you at eighty, it would seem that I was wrong." He looks at Bill and Peter.

Bill nods glumly. "Yeah, I'm forty-five. And now that you draw my attention to it, I take more sick leave than I used to. I was aware of this, but I didn't dwell on it. I also put it down to age."

Peter shrugs. "Same story." He looks at me despairingly. "I hope you have an answer to this. What can we do about it? I certainly don't want to have to look for a different job."

I smile at them. "It's okay, there is a way. A few minutes ago I mentioned the adage, where you focus, your energy flows . . . and connects. This is . . ."

"Every time you say this, you put a different tag on the end," Anita chips in. The last time it was *creates,* this time *connects*. Which is it?"

I laugh at her. "Good, you're listening! You remind me of Cheeky Hobson in *Footrot Flats*. It was my favourite cartoon series of all time."

"I've never heard of it," Anita says.

Chuckling, I nod. "Before your time. Created by Murray Ball, it was set in rural New Zealand. It was about the Dog and his owner, a guy named Wally, and his friend Cooch, and the animals on the farm. Cheeky Hobson was his girlfriend. Seriously funny if you have a farming background. It was so funny they even made a movie of it. But, I digress. Where you focus, energy flows, *and* connects, *and creates!* Okay . . . you get that. So as you do your counselling work you are focusing and creating and connecting. You get that? In every moment you are creating and connecting. However, you do get to decide what you focus on. If you focus on their problem, you connect with it and with their problematic emotional energy. Whereas if you focus on the solution, you get to connect with this and with the uplifting, healing energy that it offers. Need I say that most people focus on the problem, connecting with a descending energy, rather than the uplifting energy of the solution?"

I frown at Anita. "Do you fully comprehend what I am saying?"

She nods contritely. "Yes, I really do, and I can see *how* and *why* what you suggest will make a huge difference."

Todd and the others all nod enthusiastically.

"When you connect with the energy of the solution, or an experimental solution, or even a didn't-work solution, you are always connecting with the energy of its potential. If the solution didn't work, then it will usually indicate the way to *another* potential solution that may work. You are always working with an uplifting energy, and this means that you will not get emotionally dragged down toward sickness. Not only this, but you will enjoy the process far more, because you will be working with an uplifting energy. And when you enjoy what you are doing, you do not get sick in the way of not liking what you are doing. We are the creators of our sicknesses, our jobs can't do this."

"Not to be difficult, but what about the chemical pollution in the hairdressers shops? Surely it is their environment that makes them sick, rather than themselves," Marsha quietly says.

I smile at her. "Back to your relationship with yourself. If you actually Love yourself – and this is all too rare – and you value good health, you would not work in a hairdressers shop simply because your consciousness of self-Love would either guide you away from such work, or deny your ability to get such employment. And if you have friends in this industry, please do not think that I am belittling them, for I am not. I am simply saying that it is a dangerous environment for long-term employment. This is fairly well known and documented. People desperate for a job, or people drawn to this industry, either dismiss such misgivings, or think that it does not apply to *them*. But, of course, this happens in all high risk employment. It's the same with smoking. We have a common attitude that the health risk applies to *other* people . . . not me. Until it is too late!

"Our good health is not a given. If we want good health, then we have to create it. Nobody else can do this for us . . . and I mean *nobody*. We, alone, are responsible for our wellbeing. Today's attitude is almost the opposite to this; the health industry will look after us. Certainly the advice of *genuine* nutritionists can make a difference to our health, but ironically the only people who listen to them, or read their books and articles, are the people who are already aware of nutrition and *are* caring for themselves."

"I feel very relieved by what you have told us. I, for one, will be careful to focus toward, and on, the solution. Of course, I have been doing exactly the opposite. Thank you," Peter says, with great sincerity.

... TWENTY-EIGHT ...

Thoughts and Emotions

*The energy of our thoughts and emotions are the most
creative aspects of our lives. Our thoughts and emotions
precede every action we make. We are inclined to blame
or praise our actions in everyday life, and this is logical,
yet they are no more than the physical manifestation of
the thoughts and emotions that unwittingly preceded them.*

—Michael J. Roads

THE OTHERS ECHO HIS WORDS, thanking me with great enthusiasm.

Todd looks at me speculatively. "I find it interesting that in so much of what you have spoken about, it all seems to come down to our own thoughts and emotions. I guess you call this the metaphysical aspect."

Before I can reply, Carolyn comes walking up to where we are seated on the deck. The sun is shining into our area, warming it nicely. Personally, I enjoy being warm. Cold and shivering does not work for me.

She gives all our guests her wide, warm, heart-connected smile. "It's now late-afternoon, so if you are ready, I'll take your last orders for tea, coffee, or some more of the iced tea with mint."

155

As she receives their various requests, I reflect on the fact that the day is passing surprisingly quickly. I have connected with these five people more powerfully than I expected. I feel a sense of *deep* satisfaction in the formerly reluctant Peter's major breakthrough, and the way that the whole group is both enthusiastic and receptive.

Carolyn returns to the kitchen, and I continue with what I was about to say in reply to Todd's speculative comment.

"Yes, Todd, it's *always* the metaphysical aspect. As I keep saying, everything is energy. The energy of our thoughts and emotions are the most creative aspects of our lives. Our thoughts and emotions precede every action we make. We are inclined to blame or praise our actions in everyday life, and this is logical, yet they are no more than the physical manifestation of the thoughts and emotions that unwittingly preceded them. Imagine a typical day for a typical city person . . . if there is such a mythical person! They get up in the morning, and for many people this means turning on the TV to watch the continual news feed of CNN, or to glance at it on our smart phones while on the way to work. For me, CNN means Continuous Negative News, and I consider this an unwise way to begin the day. Some people watch this stuff with little interest, simply wanting to be able to talk about the daily news in conversation; others really connect with great worry or concern about daily politics and world events, *needing* this type of information. And so the day's emotional connections begin . . . scarcely uplifting!

"For many parents, before they even leave the house, they are in conflict with one or more of their modern know-it-all teenage kids. Another common scenario. After a brief but angry shouting match, the parent heads off to work and the kids head off to school. Both are now emotionally disturbed on a very subtle level, so it is very unlikely that any of them will recognise it. Nevertheless, this negative disturbance is going to affect the way that they each create their day. And here we have yet another seriously huge, unrecognised factor – we each create our own day! At this point in the lives of my mythical *typical* family, they have made a fairly disastrous, but very common, beginning. Everyone is just slightly disgruntled and annoyed with another member of the family.

"The kids who grow up with this regular shouting match become emotionally hardened to it, and this, in turn, has an effect on their whole lives ahead of them. These are the formative years for kids, and most parents know this, but we don't approach it with any consistent awareness. We are too busy, in too much in a hurry to be sensitive to the effects of our often hasty or thoughtless words."

I smile at them. "See . . . we are back to the power of words and their emotional content. Thoughts and emotions! All of us – and I include myself – need to be far more careful with our thoughts and the words that come from them, and we need to be more aware of the emotional value we give those words. It is the emotional value that holds the long term effect.

"Okay, so our mythical kids are at school, and the mythical parent is at work, and although none of them is actually thinking about the mornings altercation – it's too common – the energetic repercussions are within their consciousness. And what is within our consciousness affects the actions that flow from that state of consciousness. The kids at school will not take in the information of their lessons as easily, and they will be judged for it, while the parent at work will find small, trifling, aggravating errors that may creep in and disrupt his or her flow of energy in however they express it at work. One of the results of this for the parent is fatigue. Another is constant exasperation, feeling put-out, irritation, none of which is conducive to workplace efficiency or achievement. Neither is it going to forge a better relationship between husband and wife when they finally arrive home from work. The downside of this is reaching for the whisky or wine bottle. 'Just a glass to help me unwind, so I can relax!' It does not work. There is no way alcohol is going to cure an emotional problem that is re-created every day. Ten years down the track the single glass is now two or three glasses to get the same effect . . . and it so continues downhill, all too often into alcoholism."

Todd shakes his head thoughtfully. "I've never looked at everyday life like this. What I thought was misfortune and accidents and outside influences in our lives, to you is all the metaphysical aspect of our *own* creation. Why doesn't everyone know about this?" He smiles. "Timing, right?"

I grin. "Yes, but timing is all about consciousness. As we grow in consciousness, so we create our own timing. Sadly, the opposite is also true.

The more reactive we are, the more negative our thoughts and emotions, down goes our state of consciousness and the more locked-in we become to our destructive behaviour. If I spoke about this on national television, I would be mocked and ridiculed by every intellectual professional with any expertise in the area of psychology. The intellect with its ego connection is too arrogant to be humbled."

"How about the *upside* of thoughts and emotions," Marsha asks.

I chuckle. "I like that . . . and, of course, there is an upside . . . but not with our mythical *typical* family. We would need to create an equally mythical but *exceptional* family. The relationship the parents have with themselves and each other will be far more evolved than normal. They practice their skills of communication, of being considerate to others, and they are committed to the wellbeing of each other and the family. This family is sensitive to each other and to all members of the family. The parents do not shout at their kids, even if he or she feels like it on occasions. They approach the kids and discuss issues without accusations, without rights or wrongs, but offering creative ways to deal with any issues that might arise. In this way, the kids go to school feeing loved, valued and worthwhile. They are told by the parents almost daily that they are loved, and this engenders within them a sense of deep, needful, emotional security. At school they are able to focus and concentrate, so they get good grades, according to their abilities. Interestingly, the lower emotions engender a victim consciousness, often resulting in being bullied at school. This mythical *exceptional* family has kids who do not have a self-created victim consciousness, so they are not a natural target for kids from the mythical *typical* family. Like it or not . . . like attracts like!

"And so it is for the mythical exceptional parents. At work they are popular with most of their work staff, while some may be threatened by them. Oddly, the mythical typical parents are not threatening, but the mythical exceptional parents carry a different energy. It either attracts other people or it repels them, all according to the mental and emotional state of the other people. If it threatens them, it is because they are emotionally insecure; if it attracts, then obviously those attracted are reasonably emotionally secure."

Marsha gives me a shrewd look. "I would guess that the exceptional people, or family, would not have a very wide circle of friends."

I nod. "And you would be correct. Too many others are threatened by them, and they themselves are not attracted by conversational trivia or shallow people."

"Would that be a judgement?" Marsha asks.

I shake my head. "No, by their actions shall you know them. The simple reality is that birds of a feather *do* flock together. This is neither wrong or bad, it happens naturally. Nobody wants to mix with people who make them feel uncomfortable. Thoughts and emotions in action again. The mythical typical family and the mythical exceptional family would not naturally mix. And that's okay. It would probably be without judgement, in the same way that oil and water do not mix. I do not mix well with some ego-centred intellectual people. They are who they are perfectly, no judgements, but they no more want to be with me then I do with them. How perfect is that?

"Over twenty years ago I used to have problems with some of the women in my – then named – Retreats. In those days I considered the problem was about them, not me, but as it continued I was compelled to look at myself more deeply. At first I thought it was an intellectual problem, but that quickly revealed itself to be false. Gradually, I realised that these were women with whom I either had *no* emotional connection, or had an *adverse* emotional connection. They also felt the same repugnance toward me. I admit, in those days I was a long way from emotional balance! How was I to resolve this? "What I eventually did, worked. When I would meet one of these women at the beginning of a Retreat, where we each felt a mutual emotional dislike, I would make myself approach them and speak nicely to them, embracing them warmly and welcoming them to the Retreat. Mostly, they would respond, even if a bit stiff and severe. I knew that I had to deal with this, not expect that they would. And so it worked. As I freed myself from the negative emotional bonds that accompanied me, so I freed those women with whom I interacted. Only one or two did not respond, nor did I ever see them again. What is interesting is that within a few years, I no longer had this emotional reaction to certain women. It had gone . . . because I *creatively* faced it."

"Very good," says Marsha. "Most men would just blame the women, and make no move to deal with it. You took responsibility."

I nod. "Thank you, yes. I took emotional responsibility for the emotional situations that our mutual emotional prejudices created. And happily, by doing so it removed my unrealised emotional prejudices."

... TWENTY-NINE ...

The Metaphysics of Nature

When I am conscious in the garden, the Nature spirits
come close to me, touching into my consciousness with
their insights and their deep knowings. If I am conscious,
we connect. This triggers in me deeper intuitive knowing
and insights that are part of the universal All. It is, however,
a two-way exchange. From me they receive recognition
and acceptance. This is also a connection. Within my
energy-field are certain aspects of human consciousness
that benefit them, so both parties grow in the energetic
exchange.

—Michael J. Roads

I TAKE A DEEP BREATH. "So, what else do you have on your topics list?"

They all look at Todd, and Todd looks at me. "It's now late afternoon, but we have a little time yet, so what would you like to offer us? I have no doubt that it will be enlightening."

Anita chimes in. "Personally, I'm a Nature lover. So although it offers nothing regarding our work, it will definitely benefit me, and hopefully all of us. So how about something to do with Nature?"

I smile contentedly. Now we're talking! This is *my* subject. "How about the metaphysics of Nature?"

Nods all round greet my suggestion. "But what does that actually mean?" Anita asks.

"It means that nothing is quite as it appears to be. We see everything from a physical perspective and immediately assume that this is the way it is; but we are metaphysical Beings living in a greater metaphysical reality, so we see the physical reflection of Nature rather than the metaphysical reality."

Anita smiles cheekily. "Okay, I can ponder that statement for a while, or you can explain what that last bit means. Like, how can Nature be a physical reflection of something that nobody can see?"

I frown at her. "Can you see the bones in your body? No, you can't, but an X-ray machine can. Just because you can't see beyond a physical Nature does not mean that nobody can. Throughout the ages our mystics, along with many inspired poets and artists, have seen and, in their own ways, through art or poetry or prose, have attempted to share it with others. I remember long ago when I lived in Tasmania, visiting a forest that had been clear-felled for the paper industry. The devastated forest was a shameful sight, a greedy rape and plunder of Nature. I sat down on a tree stump, looking at the desolation and havoc of human greed. I had tears in my eyes. But as I looked, my vision gradually left the physical scene and somehow I was inner-seeing the greater metaphysical reality. To my shock all the forest trees were standing, the forest remaining untouched and undisturbed. It took me years to reconcile what I saw on these two levels of reality; the physical and the metaphysical. It was years before I grew into a greater understanding of the metaphysical aspect of Nature. I learned that man can ruin the physical expression, but the metaphysical is beyond our reach; especially beyond the reach of a rape-and-ruin consciousness."

Todd looks at me thoughtfully. "One of my clients lost a leg a number of years ago, and he has a prosthesis. He told me that it has short periods of terrible itching. I laughed, asking how a prosthesis could itch. He could not explain it, but insisted that the itch also happens to others like him."

I nod. "Yes, we can lose a physical limb, but metaphysically we never lose a limb. Certain stimulations affect the metaphysical limb, and then those stimulations express through the physical limb. The metaphysical precedes the physical! Remember? Despite losing a leg, he was still feeling the metaphysical itch. I think the term they have coined for this phenomenon is a phantom limb!"

I sweep my right arm around to draw their eyes toward the garden. "All that your eyes encompass is my garden. Most areas I work with, some areas I don't touch. But what you are seeing is a physical garden. It's difficult to accept or even realise that the garden you see is a physical reflection of a greater metaphysical reality. In *Through the Looking-Glass* Lewis Carroll's Alice went through the mirror into an alternate reality. Years ago I also went through the mirror image, or should I say the membrane between the physical and the metaphysical, into a greater metaphysical reality. I met no White Rabbit or Mad Hatter or Cheshire Cat or Queen of Hearts – none of that crowd – but it did reveal a world of Nature spirits, of tree devas, of elves and other mystical Beings within a realm of Nature that took my breath away."

Anita laughs. "So you believe in fairies and elves? Really?"

I smile at her. "If you met a girl your own age who had been blind since birth, and you described a Jacaranda tree in full magnificent flower to her, you would expect her to believe you. Suppose she accused you of making it up. Suppose she said that nothing could exist as amazing as your description. What would you do; what would you say?"

Anita nods contritely. "Okay, I get your point. It reminds me of the story of the man who got lost in the wilderness, and stumbled into the valley of the blind. He described to them what sight was and what it revealed. That night while he was sleeping, they bound him and, in their love and mercy, took out his eyes, hoping to take away his madness." She shivered. "That story creeps me out."

I nod. "Yes, I'm familiar with it. To answer your question, yes, I do believe in fairies and elves, and in magic and miracles. The outer areas of my garden remain undisturbed especially for the Nature spirits."

Anita looks serious. "But why? Your whole garden is surrounded by bush and forest. Isn't this enough for the Nature spirits? Why do they need some of yours?"

"A fair enough question. They do not *need* any of my garden. I do what

I do to acknowledge them and to encourage them to be close, thus we both benefit from the proximity of the other. When I am conscious in the garden, they come close to me, touching into my consciousness with their insights and their deep knowings. If I am conscious, we connect. This triggers in me deeper intuitive knowing and insights that are part of the universal All. It is, however, a two-way exchange. From me they receive recognition and acceptance. This is also a connection. Within my energy-field are certain aspects of human consciousness that benefits them, so both parties grow in the energetic exchange.

"When you are attuned to this deeper aspect of Nature you can use it to your mutual advantage. When, at the turn of this century, we entered a long period of drought in this area, I knew that I did not have enough water to keep the garden plants alive. We have only tank water here, no city water. We catch it on the roof and store it. No rain equals no water. So although I can store about two hundred thousand litres, it would not last long in watering a large garden. Anyway, as the drought took hold, I walked around my garden imagining an English winter, where all the plants are dormant in the extreme cold and wet. I showed this inner picture to the plants of my garden, telling them that we were going into a period of hot and dry. If they also dropped their leaves and went to sleep, they would survive. I told them that if they needed more energy they could take as much from me as they needed, I had plenty for all of us. Then I jokingly suggested that when the drought ended they could give it back.

"During the first two weeks all my *evergreen* plants dropped their leaves, except for my half-dozen Ixora *(West Indian Jasmine)* shrubs. They eventually withered and died. Quite honestly, the whole garden looked sick and devastated. However, all the other shrubs survived. Sure, we had plenty of brief showers, but never enough rain to soak the soil.

"The drought lasted about twenty months.

"When, finally, the deep soaking rains came, the plants did not leaf up, instead they all burst into flower around the same time . . . and the energy that literally poured off from them was amazing. I never did feel them take energy from me, but I certainly felt it when they gave it back. Incidentally, in our area most of the other gardens lost around seventy percent of the non-native species. And mine were mostly non-native."

"So you did this with a deep level of communication. I didn't know this was possible. I also like gardening," Marsha says. "Could I do such a thing under similar circumstances?"

I smile. "That depends entirely on you: your openness, your state of consciousness, your connection with Nature . . . things like that. Love is involved. Not hollow, empty, meaningless *words* of love, but the true *expression* of Love. When I was a boy, I knew a ninety-two year old woman who lived in a terraced house with a small garden surrounded by high brick walls. The garden was always shady, but her little garden was full of bright flowering plants. I was only ten, but at that age I had a large collection of about two hundred potted plants and cacti. I knew my plants, Latin names included. I knew that the plants in her garden did not have enough sun to flower, because apart from a few specialised species, sunlight is the flowering factor. It puzzled me every time I visited her garden. Then one day . . . revelation. As I watched her smiling at her tiny garden and plants, I *felt* her connection. I realised that *she was the sun* in her garden. That moment had a life-changing effect on me. In that moment I knew that when Love enters the equation, all the rules are changed. All without her conscious awareness of it, she wrote her own rules through her deep Love for her plants. That is what I *consciously* did at the beginning of the drought. It's all about energy, so I rewrote the script!

"Love is not physical. Love *can* be physically expressed, but Love is truly metaphysical. Everything on our beautiful world that endures eternity is metaphysical. Over vast periods of time the physical expressions of Nature come and go, but the metaphysical expressions are eternal. We talk of plant and animal species becoming extinct, but that is just so much nonsense. This is the infant ramblings of a species that believes in death, believes in endings. There is no death. There is no ending, any more than there is a beginning. These are games played in linear time, where we use the tools and toys of cause and effect, and polarity and duality, with which to consciously grow. God created life, *never* death. Aeons ago we made up the idea of death. We see a dead animal, or person, and we see death, the end. What we do not see with our physical senses is that life – which is inextinguishable – continues. Life is metaphysical, not physical. As I said, the Nature we see is the physical expression of eternal life. It is not life itself.

Nature is the great teacher for those with the humility to be open enough to realise this."

I pause, considering whether to share this. "Years ago when I was a farmer in Tasmania, I truly loved my herd of about a hundred milking cows, but I hated milking them. I had no idea that energetically, my hate of milking was a deep disturbance and agitation to the cows. They kicked, they shitted green liquid, they were difficult and they withheld some milk. And this mayhem lasted for two to three years. One day a long-legged Friesian cow on her way into the milking stall kicked me on my quadricep muscle. It was serious pain. I staggered around and, angrily grabbing a leg chain, I attempted to hit her (okay, I wasn't always the nice guy of today, this was a much earlier me!) and something quite unforeseen happened. As I swung the leg chain it got diverted, missed the cow's ribs, hooked onto a flailing hoof, was snatched out of my hand, and two arcs of rapidly increasing speed later it wrapped around my left arm. The pain was so shockingly bad I almost passed out. I had to have a few days off while my late wife did the milking. This was humiliating, because all was calm in the milking shed when she took over! She had a very different relationship with the cows!

"I returned after three days, although it took four months for the pain to completely go. A lasting reminder! As I began the process of milking I was aware of a huge change in me. When the chain wrapped around my arm, I *knew* in that shocking and painful moment that I was the author of my pain. It was all down to me. I *knew* that all the turmoil of milking was *my* inner turmoil. I *knew* this instantly and beyond all doubt. So now, on my return, I began milking from a changed consciousness, although I didn't know it then. The cows were quiet and cooperative. The green shit did not fly and no cows kicked or skittered. All was calm and easy. And it remained so until years later when I quit dairy farming. What is interesting is that every cow in the herd *knew* that I had changed . . . so our relationship changed. But of all my family and friends, not a single one was aware of it. I pondered that for a long time. How could cows know this and people close to me not know? Eventually, I learned that the cows and I were energetically more deeply connected at that level of consciousness, than I was with my friends. Like it or not, with a few exceptions, my human friendships were more superficial."

I laugh. "I could regale you with stories like this until tomorrow. But please remember that the depths of consciousness within Nature are not lesser than in humanity, nor vice versa, they are both very different. The streams of consciousness that are humanity and Nature are One, despite that they express differently and are moving in different directions. And yet the paradox: in a greater reality all directions are One.

"If people knew of the richness of the potential in connecting with Nature, and made that *conscious* connection, we would all benefit. But it isn't going to happen any time soon. We are still involved in the plunder and ruin mentality, like in the rape of the world's forests, the slaughter of elephants, in the killing of whales, and so it goes, on and on in the overall exploitation of Nature in thousands of different ways . . . and all to our own detriment.

"It is unfortunate that we live on this planet as such an unenlightened species, so terribly ignorant of the damaging repercussions of our actions."

. . . THIRTY . . .

Unenlightened and Enlightened

*He gives up, but he does not give in. He lets go of the
endless trying, of all the beliefs about whether it is possible
or not. He lets go of all his wants. He lets go of his spiritual
knowledge. Finally, he surrenders to the fence. Fully and totally
surrenders. His eyes are closed as tears stream down his face.
He feels as though something inside is tearing, as though his
entrails are being painlessly drawn from his belly. He feels as
though his heart is exploding. And as he surrenders to the fence,
he feels as though he is sinking deep, deep into the earth.
Everything he has strived for, is gone. He is nothing in nothing,
feeling the nothing of nothing. He is completely lost.*

—Michael J. Roads

PETER STARES AT ME THOUGHTFULLY. "Obviously there is a considerable
difference between an enlightened person and an unenlightened one. I
get this. But what I don't understand is what that difference actually is.
I realise that you are enlightened and that you see life in a very different
way, but *why* do you see it differently? What changed? I'm struggling with
this."

"Fair enough. Hmm . . . how do I explain? As an educated man, would you attempt to teach Pythagoras to a boy in kindergarten? Probably not. Without in any way diminishing you, this is what you are asking. But it's not an impossible question, not if I take poetic licence with it.

"Let's say a kindergarten boy grows up and he is programmed to seek success. He grows to be a man and he begins to tap into his soul potential. He inner-feels the hollowness of being 'successful'. His father is successful. As a child he was impressed, as an adult he sees the flaws. And as his sense of inner-exploration grows, life moves to meet this naturally developing inner inquiry. He reads new literature about life and moves on to the many books about spirituality. Either this ignites him, or it does not . . . timing! If it does, then he begins to walk a different path from the masses. His parents may not like it, but he is determined to live *his* life, not theirs, nor their expectations of his life.

"Maybe he will get lost along this new, but very old path, maybe he will find himself. But this is the path that leads toward the *inner new*, the path that opens doors that other people seldom encounter. And as he passes through these doors, so he becomes more and more distant from his fellow men. He does not create distance, yet it is the distance that is recreating him. On this path he will gain spiritual knowledge, for this is the most common of spiritual paths. Maybe he will get lost in his spiritual knowledge – many do – maybe he will learn what Kahlil Gibran meant when he wrote: '*And what is knowledge but a shadow of wordless knowledge?*' Maybe he will realise that life is for living, rather than the knowledge of what living is. The day will come when he realises that he, along with most of humanity, is rather like a chicken living in a chicken pen. The pen is huge, as big as the world, and the man realises that the fence containing chickens/humanity is high and solid and, shock, horror . . . invisible. But he can see it! He attempts to show the fence to other people and he learns that they cannot see it. He is shaken by this to the very core of his Being. Gradually he learns that he can see it because he is looking from within Self, from his pineal, while other people look through their eyes. He tells them this, all to no avail. In desperation he offers seminars on how to see the fence that encloses humanity, but he is mocked and ridiculed. He is at a loss as to how to help himself or other people. Time passes and he learns that people don't care about being enclosed simply because they do not *experience* it. He is enclosed because he feels it and experiences it. They do not. What a paradox. What can he do? Ah yes, he must escape from the vast, enclosed chicken pen.

"He meditates. He does advanced yoga postures. He endlessly reads spiritual literature. But this all seems so slow and he is getting older. Along the way he fell in love and got married, but now he is alone. His wife was a normal woman, wanting the normal womanly things in life. They parted and divorced amicably. He is now a rather solitary man, for few people understand the deep and terrible longing that drives him. One day, he realises that, as big as the fence is, it has been steadily moving closer and closer to him – or has he been getting closer and closer to the fence? He realises that it does not matter. As he stares at the fence, he sees a tiny, tiny flaw in the structure of the fence. He takes out a pocket knife and attempts to make the tiny flaw bigger, but as soon as he uses the knife, the flaw is gone, the structure fully sealed. He tries all manner of other tools, but always with the same result.

"Finally, after a few years of trying to make the tiny flaw bigger, he gives up. He sits and patiently stares at the tiny flaw. Now he probes at it with his consciousness, not to understand, but to connect. He connects consciously with the huge fence. Over a long period of time, he realises that the fence has no actual structure. He stares at the flaw, connecting. More years pass by and one day he reaches an inner crisis. He is in trouble. He has allowed life to pass him by. He is ill. He is weakened. He is in pain. He decides that he will give up. It is not possible to get through the fence. Maybe he is insane, or completely deluded. Maybe it is not the other people who are imprisoned, but him, imprisoned by his delusions. He surrenders his search. Twenty years have passed him by and he is as imprisoned in this moment as he ever has been. He thinks of all the many books that he has read, of all the spiritual knowledge that he has acquired . . . what good has it done him? None at all. As he sits before the fence none of it makes the slightest difference. All the knowledge in his head cannot make the tiny flaw one fraction bigger.

"Finally, he gives a huge sigh. He gives up . . . but he does not give *in*. He lets go of the endless trying, of all the beliefs about whether it is possible or not. He lets go of all his wants. He lets go of all the spiritual knowledge. Finally, he surrenders to the fence. Fully and totally surrenders. His eyes are closed as tears stream down his face. He feels as though something inside is tearing, as though his entrails are being painlessly drawn from his belly. He feels as though his heart is exploding. And as he surrenders to the fence, he feels as though he is sinking deep, deep into the earth. Everything he has strived for is gone. He is nothing in nothing, feeling the nothing of nothing. He is completely lost.

"Timeless time passes . . . he opens his eyes.

"There is no fence. He blinks, staring all around, but there is no fence. He realises that he is now on his feet, no pain, no sickness, no weakness. A Light is shining onto, and into, him. He feels as though he is being held in the arms of Love. He is smiling. He sees a sight that is lost to the sight of normal people. A world of startling beauty. Incredible, extraordinary beauty. A woman and a man that he knows walk past him, looking at him with pity. But they are acquaintances rather than friends, so there are no words between them; but he is shocked. This couple are both facially deformed and have been most of the lives. In the silence of his thoughts, he thought of them as the ugly couple and had felt shame for such thoughts. Now, as he glances at them, he is astonished to see their beauty. Physically, their faces are exactly the same, but they are truly beautiful. He has learned that it is the viewer who creates beauty. There is nothing that is not beautiful when the consciousness of beauty has merged with your own inner consciousness.

"And so he begins to adjust to life. He has learned of timing, of Truth. He laughs. He *is* Truth, yet he spent ages looking for it. He *is* beauty, yet he saw it only in flowers and pretty girls. He *was* the fence, yet he saw it outside of himself. It was only with surrender that he no longer created the fence. What a paradox, he and all humanity create the fence, yet attempting to get through the fence maintains its reality. He now sees and knows that the world is perfect. Everyone is in their perfect place in the perfect moment learning their most perfect lesson. The criminal waiting to be executed is about to learn the immortality of life . . . again! The billionaires with their vast wealth are learning the futility of material attachments . . . again! The sick and starving masses in the Third World countries are learning that poverty thinking creates a life of poverty . . . again! The elderly sick are learning that age and sickness do not have to coexist . . . again! All the thousands that are dying in each moment are learning that even in the zest of life in the illusion, they were dying . . . again! They are learning that death is the doorway to life, just as birth is the doorway to death . . . again! All the people lost in their self-created apathy are learning that it does not work for them . . . again! And so it is, on and on.

"The man is experiencing enlightenment. He smiles as he realises that it means quite simply; In-Light-it-meant. Most of humanity lights candles in the dark and as the light flickers eerily, it creates more fear. The man no longer has any relationship with fear. He is immortal, as is all humanity. He no longer lives from action and reaction. He allows life to express through him, for he is life and he is the expression. The huge weight of worry and anxiety has gone, along with all his criticism and judgement of himself and the world. He is filled with peace. He chuckles, because he knows peace is an experience that can never be understood, for the closed mind can never experience it! He lives in a greater reality and he is more aware than ever of the weight of the limitations and expectations that accompany the ordinary person on their eternal journey into life. He feels saddened by the illusions under which so very many people live. He is aware that his relationship with himself has undergone a tremendous change; a change so profound that it changes his whole relationship with the world. He is now aware of himself as Self, the eternal Being, as well as self, the mortal identity. They are One, yet people live their lives with a mortal focus, rather than a greater, immortal focus.

"And so he faces his first quandary. The world is perfect and everyone is in their perfect place in life; a place that they have each created. He feels that he would like to help humanity, but he also realises that most of humanity has no idea that it needs help. He hesitates. Does he offer the world his new insight, or not? He spends weeks engaging life with the enquiry of his new quandary.

One day, in his garden, he is looking at the beauty of a flower. He is marvelling because although it is the same flower on the same plant each year, yet it is *never* the same. It is a *new* flower, with a *new* energy. Nature does not indulge in sameness; that is a human occupation. He Loves all the flowers. And as he stares at the flower, it comes to him that all the flowers of the world have to be pollinated each year, otherwise, over a period of time, there would be no more flowers. And this, too, would be perfect. But in his Love for the flowers, he clearly sees the answer to his quandary. As they unfold and open, he will pollinate human flowers with Joy and Truth and Beauty, with unconditional Love and Light. He will do it in their own perfect timing, for the choice will always be theirs."

I smile at the group as they listen, spellbound.

"The end . . . of the beginning."

In Closing . . .

AFTER ALL THEIR HUGS HAVE BEEN SHARED and their heartfelt appreciation spoken, and with echoes of 'I'll see you at the next Intensive' ringing in my ears, the house feels suddenly quiet and empty.

I muse over how they all endeared themselves to me. Peter with his initial hostility was in tears at his departure. Todd, more with it from the start, and Bill, were both profoundly moved. Moved as in changed. Marsha now considers that her *real* life is about to begin and Anita . . . I chuckle, she swore that she would be back in a few weeks. She loves both Carolyn and me, and wants to spend more time with us. I smile. We will see!

Walking across to our bookcase in the lounge, I idly pull out a copy of *The Prophet,* by Kahlil Gibran. As I hold it, the pages fall open on his words about Love. I read it once again, breathing in the fragrance of his Truth. And again I ponder the miracle that, while the use of words and style may date and age, the wisdom contained remains as fresh as the moment of its birth.

As I read, I decide, as a tribute, to have Kahlil Gibran share his Truth at the closing of a beautiful day. And nothing could be more appropriate than his words on Love. I have lived and experienced Love so often in the manner that he describes, for even as Love crowned me, so too it crucified me, and Love most certainly directs my course in life. True, I did not expect any of this, but Love is an eternal dynamic that transforms, not a passive kiss that has but a single, brief moment of life.

Speak to us of Love.

And he raised his head and looked upon the people, and there fell a stillness upon them. And with a great voice he said:

When Love beckons to you, follow him, though his ways are hard and steep.

And when his wings enfold you yield to him, though the sword hidden among his pinions may wound you.

And when he speaks to you believe in him, though his voice may shatter your dreams as the north wind lays waste to the garden.

For even as Love crowns you so shall he crucify you. Even as he is for your growth so he is for your pruning.

Even as he ascends to your height and caresses your tenderest branches that quiver in the sun, so shall he descend to your roots and shake them in their clinging to the earth.

Like sheaves of corn he gathers you unto himself.

He threshes you to make you naked.

He sifts you to free you from your husks.

He grinds you to whiteness.

He kneads you until you are pliant.

And then he assigns you to his sacred fire, that you may become sacred bread for God's sacred feast.

All these things shall Love do unto you that you may know the secrets of your heart, and in that knowledge become a fragment of life's heart.

But if in your fear you would seek only Love's peace and Love's pleasure, then it is better for you that you cover your nakedness and pass out of Love's threshing floor into the season-less world where you shall laugh, but not all of your laughter, and weep, but not all of your tears.

Love gives naught but itself and takes naught but from itself.

Love possesses not nor would it be possessed.

For Love is sufficient unto Love.

When you Love you should not say, 'God is in my heart,' but rather, 'I am in the heart of God.'

And think not that you can direct the course of Love, for Love, if it finds you worthy, directs your course.

Love has no other desire other than to fulfil itself.

But if you Love and must needs have desires, let these be your desires:

To melt and be like a running brook that sings its melody to the night.

To know the pain of too much tenderness.

To be wounded by your own understanding of Love; and to bleed willingly and joyfully.

To wake at dawn with a winged heart and give thanks for another day of loving; to rest upon the noon hour and meditate Love's ecstasy; to return home at eventide with gratitude; and then to sleep with a prayer for the Beloved in your heart and a song of praise upon your lips.

—Kahlil Gibran

ABOUT MICHAEL J. ROADS

Michael Roads was born a farmer's son in Cambridgeshire, England, in 1937. From an early age he discovered that he had a natural ability to travel beyond linear time and space, and enter into deep communication with Nature. Since his spiritual enlightenment at age 49, Michael has written 21 books on his experiences and many explorations of alternate realities and dimensions. His main focus and teachings are based in *unconditional* Love and emotional balance.

The year 2017 marks his 26th year of traveling over five continents presenting inspirational and life-changing 5-Day Intensives in a clear, compelling, humorous and no-nonsense format, enabling many participants to experience profound shifts in consciousness.

Michael, a modern mystic, weaves his wealth of life experiences with the most extraordinary insights – insights that offer pathways to our deep spiritual relationship with Nature and with Self. He has both the consciousness and the ability to empower people to gain understanding of the true nature of reality, and assist them in their spiritual awakening to their Divine potential.

For the international tour schedule and additional information please visit . . . www.michaelroads.com

RoadsLight Pty Ltd
P.O. Box 778
Nambour, QLD 4560
Australia
office@michaelroads.com

SIX DEGREES PUBLISHING GROUP
"Books that Transcend the Ordinary"

CPSIA information can be obtained
at www.ICGtesting.com
Printed in the USA
BVOW09s1209201117
500905BV00003B/429/P